A Lioness

A Lioness

Published by Michelle Camm, 2022

Instagram: @michellecamm2020

ISBN 978-1-7397659-0-3

Typesetting and cover design by The Book Typesetters
us@thebooktypesetters.com
07422 598 168
www.thebooktypesetters.com

A Lioness

My story of cancer, courage, love and friendship

Michelle Camm

Life is the ultimate prize
and
living is the lottery win

Never let your grey matter limit your dreams

"I'm spreading my wings, my darling"

Dedications

I dedicate this book to my hero — my husband Richard. Your strength is relentless. When you're not by my side my heart is incomplete.

My two lumps of titanium — my teenagers. Trinity, you are the most loyal female friend I have. You have the kindest heart. Owen, you are my sunshine whenever I am with you.

My friends, new and old. Your keyboard responses have been my kisby ring.

My very golden friend, Martina. Our bond is till the end of time.

Contents

Prologue

This is a story of how I coped,
lived life and kept a positive attitude.

I went for regular cervical screenings and did all I could to avoid cancer. My most recent smear check was in January 2020, and the results from this appointment gave me the re-assurance that I was healthy, and that cancer was in no way an issue. Little did I know!

Around 14 days after receiving the "all clear" from my screening check-up, on two separate occasions I witnessed tiny shows of blood after intercourse. Because I'd physically held a letter only weeks previous saying that my screening was normal, I dismissed these incidents as insignificant and thought that the two bleeds were being caused by my husband aggravating the area that the nurse had scraped badly on my cervix. The nurse had apologised for the discomfort that she had inflicted on my insides to obtain a good swab sample for the screening process.

My body finally waved its danger flag and I experienced a terrifying sign! Now my body meant business and scared the hell out of me. Blood was everywhere. This was after intercourse on 16th May 2020. This really worried me. This happened roughly 12 weeks after I had been informed by post that my smear test was negative.

On 16th June I was booked in for a colposcopy (a camera to look at the cervix area), and in the same check-up this led to a biopsy being taken from my cervix. This all took place at the Royal Derby Hospital. The biopsy haunted my thoughts. Why did the hospital feel the need to do this? What had they spotted?

On 3rd July, an oncologist informed me that I had cervical cancer with an 80% chance of beating the disease — this was frightening enough at the time.

Only six days later, on 9th July, I returned to the hospital to be told that my cancer was very late stage and aggressive. It was in my iliac lymph node, which sits near your hip — this node was four times the size that it should have been. The cancer had also settled deep in my pelvic wall area, as well as my cervix. I was informed that the tumour inside my cervix was the size of a ping-pong ball. I now had a much lower chance of survival! I started a radical treatment of chemotherapy and radiotherapy five days after hearing this terrifying news.

Some parts of my journey are terribly in-depth, but I've offered this as I really want you to shadow me; to shadow my experience. Likewise, there are some events in the book that some readers will find emotional; however, I feel I have to include them as they form such a vital part of my cancer experience and have shaped me into the woman I am today.

Here we go — you are opening the door into a cancer survivor's mindset.

I absolutely cherish the thought that any paragraph of this book may inspire someone's outlook on life.

Step aboard my roller-coaster — it's quite a ride, I promise!

How Quickly Cancer Appeared

My smear test was due in late December 2019 but, because I was on my period, the check-up was delayed until mid-January 2020. The nurse who took the smear test sample said that my cervix and everything else that she could see looked totally healthy.

In the first week of February 2020 my screening results arrived via post. The letter informed me that there were no concerning issues found, although the sample from the smear screening had flagged up a virus called HPV; at the time, reading these words alone scared me! I knew nothing about HPV and its dangers. This virus can cause abnormal cells to grow on the cervix. This I researched, shortly after putting down the letter.

The letter stated that my next appointment would be in one year's time to check that abnormalities were not occurring. Little did I know that my January 2020 smear screening was not looking for cancer — the screening looks for pre-cancerous cells; i.e. abnormal cells that grow on the cervix.

This very important piece of information about the smear test not looking for cancer was shared by my oncologist at a review meeting that my husband and I later attended. All women who have cervical cancer get their records reviewed, and this is when I asked how I could have received the all-clear from my smear screening and then only a few weeks later witness subtle signs that a tumour was growing in my cervix! I was totally mystified how only HPV had been detected! My slide was viewed in the lab and then a letter was sent out to me saying "See you in a year" — this letter had indicated that I was healthy! My cervical screening had not detected stage 3 aggressive cancer.

On 17th February 2020, shortly after I learnt of the HPV dangers my body was carrying, I had a small show of blood after sex. I blamed this on the recent smear test, where the nurse had scraped me quite badly. She had said as she took my smear sample, "Sorry if this hurts a little but it's to gain a good sample for the lab."

At the end of February, the same thing happened again — a small bleed. Again, I blamed my smear sample being taken. The two bleeds I've already mentioned were literally a thumbnail-sized show of blood; it didn't seem anything too worrying, and I thought that during intercourse my husband was rubbing up against the area the nurse had scraped.

My husband and I decided not to engage in any bedroom fun for one month to give my cervix a chance to recover. I spoke to my friend Traysi about the issue, and she suggested the above advice: to let my insides heal. I thought that this was a good suggestion. We had no sex in March. I had no bleeds. I thought I was on the right track and that the respite from intercourse was proving a success.

April unfolded and there were no issues — bedroom fun was

back to normal. I was confident that I would not experience any more signs of blood again. We were having regular fun and hadn't witnessed a single untoward moment. On 29th April though, and at 11 p.m., I had another scare. This time it was nothing related to sex — I went for a wee and wiped blood. I thought this was my period starting, but the next day there was no period. I thought this was a little odd, so I noted it on my calendar as a weird experience. Nothing alarming then happened until 16th May 2020. This is when a huge bleed occurred during sex. Blood was everywhere, fresh red blood all over me. I was extremely worried — this wasn't normal. I stood in my downstairs bathroom washing away all the blood from the insides of my legs, trying to make sense of what was happening to me. My husband was covered in blood too, from me. He tried to calm me down by remarking, "It's surely something simple; try not to worry." His reassurance didn't comfort me, but I finally dropped to sleep.

The next day couldn't come round quick enough. I clock-watched until the clock on the dining room wall read 9 a.m. I picked up the phone and called my doctor's practice. I told my GP every piece of my alarming personal encounter. She didn't seem worried and said, "Mrs Camm, your recent smear test was normal."

Her very words were, "Don't worry, Mrs Camm; it could be many things causing bleeding." Her voice reassured me as I listened to her ideas on the matter down the handset. "See you in two weeks," she said, "and in the meantime, pop for swabs and a few blood tests."

This advice I followed. At the end of May I visited the surgery, where my GP examined my cervix and didn't seem concerned. As she viewed me internally, she said, "It all looks fine apart from a few white spots on the cervix." My GP referred me to the Royal Derby Hospital for a more thorough cervical check-up called a colposcopy; this is a camera looking at a detailed image of the cervix.

My GP had also assured me as I walked into her consultation room that the blood tests — all three samples she had requested — were all fine and showing no issues. These I'd had taken a week previous at the doctor's surgery. It is a complete mystery to me to this day how these blood tests didn't detect stage 3 cancer in my bloodstream.

On returning home, I read up on the internet about the GP's finding of white spots on the cervix, and was alarmed to discover that this could be a sign of cancer! This was very concerning. What I had found out on the internet unsettled me greatly! I didn't share the information that I had discovered with anybody. It was my personal secret; I didn't want to scare everyone that knew of my problem.

The colposcopy took place on 16th June 2020, which was just over two weeks after attending my local GP practice. At this very appointment the colposcopy at the Royal Derby Hospital unearthed that a biopsy would be required. This is when I knew I was in trouble — they had spotted something gruesome. Why else do a biopsy?

On 3rd July my husband and I drove to the Royal Derby Hospital full of fear and dread. We hoped and prayed for the news that it would be an easy fix. This was four days before my son's 17th birthday. We arrived at the hospital and, because of the Covid-19 pandemic, I had to go and sit in the waiting room by myself. My brilliant rock and best friend, my husband, had to wait in the corridor outside the waiting area.

There were two ends to the Gynaecology department. These were marked by two double doors on a long wide corridor. I sat and waited by myself, terrible thoughts running through my mind, somehow knowing that after today's results, my life was never going to be the same again, no matter what my biopsy had discovered. I had high suspicions that it was going to be serious — why else would they have taken sample tissue from my cervix three weeks previous?

I had been reading up about my symptoms; it didn't fill me with confidence. I kept these deep concerns to myself, as I have said. I felt so well, and the only symptoms that were present were on-and-off displays of pinkish discharge when going to the toilet. I was not bleeding; I felt really healthy. I was just having to try and keep busy and keep my mind from caving in to the fear that I might have cancer. I'd read on the internet that bleeding during and after intercourse was a sign of late-stage cervical cancer. This is exactly what I had experienced after intercourse on 16th May.

Flick back to the waiting area on 3rd July 2020. The hands on the clock moved slowly; many ladies' names were being called, but not mine. Reception had informed me on arrival that my doctor was running 30 minutes behind schedule. I desperately wanted some news, and swiftly. Sitting and waiting on my own for my name to be called was my first test of strength; my cancer journey had begun but I was not yet aware of this.

The nurse had spoken to me at check-in and said that somebody would fetch my husband from outside the corridor when it was my turn to see the doctor. My name was called, and I followed a nurse who then said, "Wait here, I'll find your husband for you." She vacated via the double doors to find my support, my husband, but she couldn't locate him. Richard wasn't answering her calls, and she came back through the doors without my rock and friend! She asked a colleague of hers to find my husband as we walked to the doctor's room. Her colleague returned empty-handed too though.

This was all in the space of about four minutes. The nurse asked if I wanted to go back to the waiting room area and sit down until they could find Richard. I replied, "No, let's just get on with it!" The waiting for the news had taken its toll and I just couldn't wait any longer. With a heavy heart, myself and this friendly nurse who had been trying to locate Richard walked into a private consultation room. Opposite me sat a doctor who informed me that the biopsy had found cancer in my cervix, and I was going to need treatment. I asked, "How could this possibly be? I have only recently been for my smear test!" The doctor informed me that I had been carrying cancer for a long time! I was extremely shocked.

My world crumbled in a split second. My only dumbfounded reaction was "Right, okay." I displayed no emotion. My husband then came into the doctor's room; he had been waiting at the other end of the corridor. A totally innocent mistake. Richard looked straight at me as he entered the room, but I exhibited no expression of what the doctor had just revealed to me.

My rock and best friend sat down next to me and reached for my hand. I held it tight as the doctor repeated the black news to my husband. We were bowled over. We were silent; we couldn't believe the biopsy had discovered cancer — I looked a picture of health. The whole time I was sat on a chair thinking, this is nuts, I've only just recently attended my smear check-up and had a letter saying that I'm totally healthy!

The nurse led us into another consultation room where she spoke about many treatments. Her words were that I would most likely have to have a hysterectomy. The nurse said that the hospital thought that I had at least a 1B cancer. I asked what grade; I had been reading all about cancer every night since my biopsy.

Boom! She crushed my heart with her one swift reply. It was a dagger to my heart. "Grade 3," she said. As I looked at her lips moving, I was thinking back to my research. I had discovered that grade 3 was unpredictable and the most aggressive. The very worst one that exists! That's when the tears came; I couldn't stop crying. My world and my life were never going to be the same again. My husband was sitting beside me, unaware of the cancer grading system.

All I could think of whilst I sat on the chair breaking down was, "My beautiful children and husband... I'm going to die." We walked out of the department holding hands. I was walking away from my health, and it was devastating. We exited the hospital. I was an emotional wreck. My husband ran to fetch the car. Straight away I called my sister and ruined her day.

It seemed serious then on 3rd July: stage 1B, grade 3. The nurse informed me that I would need an MRI and detailed body scan at another local hospital to see if the cancer had spread to my major organs. It was all very frightening and a lot to come to terms with. I attended the City Hospital, Nottingham, to have detailed body scans between the dates of 3rd and 6th July.

On 9th July, myself and Richard both attended the Royal Derby Hospital to receive the detailed MRI scan findings. On this visit the doctor had a full picture of my disease. The doctor informed us both that the cancer hadn't spread to my major organs. We were so happy and relieved as we sat there. I smiled at my husband. A short lapse of time passed as we sat and waited for the doctor to start telling us about the hysterectomy they'd originally suggested that I would probably have to have.

I wish! Out came more devastating news from the doctor's mouth: "Mrs Camm, your cancer is a lot more serious than we first expected. It is actually a 3C cancer, and we say the "C" because it is also in one of your lymph nodes."

"Radical treatment is what we intend to do for your cancer," the doctor said. "Chemotherapy, radiotherapy and a procedure called brachytherapy. If you respond well to the chemotherapy and radiotherapy, then brachytherapy will be the last treatment." I felt so defeated. I felt there was no hope, I felt like that was the end for me in this world. I was also stunned that the doctor was suggesting that brachytherapy would only be possible for me if the other two treatments were successful. It was frightening to accept that the doctor was forewarning me that I might not even get far enough to receive this invasive procedure called brachytherapy.

My hopes of getting over 1B cancer were now in the gutter. Now I felt that there was a bloody mountain to climb barefooted! It was horrendous. We were silent; the car ride home was like a funeral procession. The car came to a halt as we arrived home. I felt the loss of my mam was unfolding all over again, but it was my life this time on the line due to cancer. My kids, I thought. They're going to see me in a coffin earlier, much earlier than I'd ever imagined. My mind was smothered by this image.

It was a complete nightmare, the pace at which my whole family had to accept that death could be on the cards for me, and the speed at which the rocket launched its danger towards us. On 3rd July I thought I had an 80% chance of survival and on 9th July my survival rate was lowered even more. In the space of six days our family had to accept that I'd got cancer, with a high chance that treatment might fail.

On Monday 13th July the hospital invited me to attend a meeting to talk about chemotherapy treatment. This is the point at which the nurse informed me that I was booked in for chemotherapy the next day! Literally within 24 hours I would be starting my journey. I sat there on the chair, stunned but grateful for the swiftness of my oncologist's request. The next day, Tuesday 14th July, I was sitting in a hospital chair, a cancer patient with a cannula in my hand, the chemotherapy introducing itself along my suffering veins. It was crazy. Once the hospital had viewed my MRI, the treatment plan was a matter of great urgency!

Telling my kids and family was heart-breaking; it was so hard to find any appropriate words that would make it seem less scary.

There were none. For the next two weeks I was in total hell; I'm not even sure how I managed to get through the days to be honest, but we all do somehow when tragedy strikes. Every waking minute I thought of cancer. Every waking minute I didn't know how I was going to accept this mammoth task. Writing it all down makes me do a massive sigh; I can't believe that I'm living to tell the tale. My closest family — Richard, my children and my in-laws — took the route of holding back tears and showing how strong they could be in front of me. I wondered how they managed to do this, but I was so grateful that they demonstrated such a solid dam.

The monstrous news came on a Friday, and then it was the weekend, the longest one I've ever known. It was absolutely bonkers. My body, oh my goodness, it had hidden cancer so well! A massive bleed only on 16th May and now it was 14th July and I was looking at a chemotherapy drip. I went to chemotherapy on my own. The first time, you can take support with you, but I saw no point in wasting six hours of my husband's busy day. I came home from my first chemo session and mowed the lawn! I pill-popped the anti-sickness tablets that the nurses on the chemo ward had administered to me; these were to keep the sickness urges at bay. The next day I felt fine. It was weird.

Through the weeks I worked as usual. My neighbours and my family were stunned. So was I. Could this be beginner's luck? I wondered. Every week passed and there I was, tip-top! Apart from the raging 3C cancer, of course. It was surreal. I would go to sleep crying about my cancer and wake up doing the same thing. I just couldn't see a way out. My darling husband would bring me a cup of tea in bed and say to me, "Oh, don't cry." There was no escaping this horrible mess, apart from by having terrible chemicals introduced into my body.

Tears were in abundance for the majority of the evenings in the first week; I just couldn't believe my bad luck. Keeping busy was the only thing that kept my cheeks dry.

The flowers flooded in; my dining table looked like a flower shop. People cared and they were loving. The blooms in the vases blessed my house with perfume and beauty but the sight of them did nothing for my heart and mood. It was my friends' and family's only way of making their contribution; they all felt so rocked and helpless. Every step taken in my house was with fear and thoughts of black, and there was no treatment plan in the very first week, which was very hard to deal with. The hospital was only able to roughly guess my cancer diagnosis and I was given many leaflets along with a thick booklet to educate myself on what was happening inside my cervix.

This, though, was when I thought the cancer was stage 1B and less of a threat. Little did I know, that first week, that my body was actually the host for late stage 3 aggressive cancer! The 168 hours of no plan, a broken heart and reading all about cervical cancer when I couldn't sleep through the nights enabled my mind to become very worried but well informed. The more my mind dug for information, the less it helped. As I used my shovel to dig deep into the internet website pages and forums, the pile of dirt I was creating was becoming a mountain beside me.

The Bomb

When I found out my cancer was stage 3C on 9th July 2020, I was devastated, heartbroken, stunned. My world was totally rocked and everyone who loved me felt the same. Having to tell all of the people who loved and cared for me that I had cancer was the worst outcome anybody could have wished for. The bleeding was down to a tumour in my cervix, and the cancer cells were making my vaginal wall weak.

With a very broken, dull heart and red eyes from extreme amounts of crying, I walked into my bedroom. It was time to sleep, or so my body clock told me. I looked at our marital bed. How the hell was I going to be able to sleep? To be able to cover myself over with the duvet, lie beside my amazing husband, my best friend, and be able to close my eyes and get some rest?

My fears were correct; I could not sleep, nor settle. The one thing that I could do well though was flood my feather pillow with uncontrollable tears that rolled down my temples. I was a total mess. I couldn't sleep. My flattened heart and soul rose out of bed and I wandered into my lonely living room on my own. My chair cuddled me. God, I'd hit the lowest point I had ever experienced.

The next day, as a couple, we discussed the day's plans. We

decided to go to work and keep busy. We arrived at our printing clothing unit.

The emotions I was experiencing were horrendous. Totally gutted, frightened, and my mood the lowest I'd ever known. I would just walk round crying my eyes out. I was inconsolable, as you can imagine, now 24 hours on from hearing that my cancer was so serious. I turned up at work in my PJs, dressing gown and slipper boots; I had no energy or desire to get dressed. The stuffing from my body had been well and truly torn out of me.

I felt on that day that I was going to live in my bed clothes for months; there didn't seem any point in even getting dressed. This was a Saturday, the day after receiving the life-changing news.

I walked to the French doors of the workroom where we produce our orders. I looked forwards and there they were: 150 leavers' hoodies, all half-started for three separate schools; tables stacked high with all different coloured hoodies. It was another stab in the heart to witness this sight. How the hell was I going to climb this other mountain too, alongside accepting late-stage cancer? I didn't want to print at all, never mind finish 150 hoodies.

Year 6 school leavers were relying on me to receive their hoodie, and those 150 school children didn't know of my torment. I couldn't let them down. My broken heart and poor health, they would never know of. I stood there pressing the hoodies. Every minute of every hour thinking about cancer in my body. I didn't feel strong. I didn't know how strong I was going to be. I didn't know if my body would reward me, but it bloody did. My mind and body together became a tremendous warrior — these are the only words to describe how well they carried me through. As I pressed each hoodie, the doctor's voice rang in my ears: "Mrs Camm, you have stage 3C cancer. We need to start radical treatment straight away."

My mum and dad, my in-laws of 21 years, came to the work unit to see how we were doing. What could they say to their daughter-in-law who had just been told that she had cancer? My father-in-law hugged me and I broke down in tears; I couldn't stop the tears flowing. I sobbed like a little girl. I wanted my mam but she was not here for me; she was high in heaven, only able to look down on me and send me strength.

As my father-in-law hugged me, he stood consoling me. I said, "I'm not ready to meet my mam yet." My face wouldn't know the normality of dry cheeks for at least another two weeks. My in-laws have always been incredibly loving and supportive, and I would like to personally thank them both for treating me like their own daughter. Kate and David Camm, you have been such fantastic parents over the 21 years that I have loved your son. I hope you read this book and are proud of me, and please just skip the chapters that make you feel uncomfortable because of such personal detail.

Over the next few days, I managed to complete the leavers' hoodies, my husband often remarking how well I was doing to push on with them. I remember having a quick break from printing and having a cup of tea and just sobbing my eyes out. The only other time I had felt this desperate and helpless was 17 years previous when my mam passed away. My heart felt as though it was dragging behind me, as if it was tied around my waist on a belt and I was walking across a riverbed of nails.

The days and nights seemed to drag and were unbearably tough. I was in a place of despair; the worry, the tears, and the gut-wrenching thoughts. The first few weeks weren't much of an improvement either. Every day went at snail pace. Every minute that was forced upon me offered thoughts of cancer and death.

The worst possible problem imaginable and my only option was to wait and see if the treatment could save my life. The total lack of control was hard to endure. This news was the hardest battle I'd ever had to cope with. The not knowing what the future had in store for me was difficult to accept. I had no choice though; I had to go with the flow and take each day one step at a time.

My husband would say, "Come to bed," and I would oblige, but sleep was not possible. My husband would cuddle me, then he'd drop to sleep so drained from the worry and the long days that we were experiencing. I would lie there crying quietly, then I'd creep out of bed so that my husband could gain some well-deserved rest. He was my rock and support every day. He was a true tower of strength, and it was a very demanding, draining job for him to witness me in such a pit of despair.

Thoughts ran through my mind of having to leave my teenage children and husband behind. It was a total living nightmare. I would sit on my own in the early hours of the morning reading leaflets. I would visit Google for information. The hours would drag. Cancer showed me how long one night takes to pass. We actually sleep for so long through the night; the 8 or 9 hours that we sleep in our bed, comfy and warm, is a mighty long time.

Being awake until 4 a.m. really dragged. The quiet of the empty living room was horrid. I didn't put the TV on, I just sat on my own thinking, "What the hell am I going to do about this?"

After the second week, the tears through the days had dried up. There were going to be no more displays of sadness if I could help it — this was my goal. My mindset had switched. My brain came to the conclusion that sadness was not going to appear on the table if my personality and emotions could work together. I also reached the quick conclusion that not sleeping was doing my body great harm. I made it my goal not to worry once my head hit the pillow — this would give my body the best chance to prepare for treatment. My eyelids dropped down and I dreamt away eight hours of fear.

The workdays never stopped; I was keen to keep my mind occupied. My aim was for life to stay normal. I was desperate and intent on not letting cancer smother me. It was later in the evenings that were the battle; the less busy times were really challenging. Nipping to our downstairs bathroom to have a brief cry for about 30 seconds was my only release when my family were around. The downstairs bathroom is just off our kitchen, and there I would dash to have a quick cry. I would think, "Pull yourself together, Michelle! Crying isn't going to send the cancer away." I'd then be okay again.

Along my journey there was one regular habit that I couldn't give up. The downstairs shower cubicle was my confession room where my gravest inner anxieties about dying could be let loose and my family not be harmed or scarred by my weeping. The tiles and the bifold glass door were the only objects that witnessed my terror. It quickly became very apparent to me that I would have to recruit a partner to muffle my sorrow, so my favourite song made its debut on my playlist and from that night on it rescued me when cancer clenched at my heart. I would re-join my family after having my shower, all of them blissfully unaware of my routine. Every day my mind would think, "Is this the day I'll take a turn for the worse?" but thank goodness that day never came. I am proud of how I handled each day, and I am proud of my kids and husband too. It has been heart-wrenchingly worrying.

All Of Me

At the age of 16, my hobby was floristry: making paper flowers in my bedroom, turning them into pretty basket arrangements for my mam and grandma. This I loved doing so much. I had dreams of becoming an interior designer, although straight from leaving school, I became a florist. I worked at my first floristry job for four years.

The two bosses that I worked for loved retail therapy and whilst they were out getting their shopping fixes, they would leave me with the responsibility of running their shop. This I took great pleasure in.

At the age of 21, having left this position, things improved greatly. I went to work at a beautiful flower stall in the Victoria Centre market in Nottingham. This new job filled me with the confidence that I could undoubtedly have a business of my own one day. Floristry was my love.

My grandma sadly passed away and left me £2,000. This was now my big opportunity to become my own boss and call the shots myself. This situation, along with my own savings, prompted me to go for it and open my own shop in Ilkeston town centre on the main high street next to a busy post office. I loved this part of my life — the freedom and the great feeling it gave me. My hard work shone. I was only 22 at this point in my life. This was my passion for the next five years. During this time, I met my husband and we had two children. When my son was six months old though, I found the 5 a.m. starts impossible, and the journeys to the flower markets early in the mornings and feeding my son bottles of milk didn't go hand in hand. Sadly, I decided to sell on my little shop to a staff member who worked for me at the time. The shop is still a thriving florists even to this day, run by my very dear friend Lisa, who was chief bridesmaid at my wedding.

When my children, Trinity and Owen, were at infant school, my next new business venture came when I started making children's birthday cakes. Everyone would remark on how good the birthday cakes looked that I had created. So, I thought, why not have a go at this as a business? The snowball grew fast, and before I knew it I was making five cakes every weekend. Again, this was another business that I was thrilled to call my own, as it offered something totally different and involved skill and creativity.

Then the BMX dream came along. When our children were 8 and 6½ years old, myself and my husband decided to open up a BMX bike shop. Our two young children at the time were talented little BMX racers; this was their hobby. Our children had been racing for about two years at this point. BMX was my husband's passion too, so I encouraged him to follow his dream and become self-employed. Together we opened a high-street shop in our hometown. We had the shop for nine years. It was tough going, juggling two young children and a shop, but we managed. It made us all pull together; it made us a super-strong family unit.

We ran a makeshift stall of BMX products at weekend BMX meetings. I loved this; I loved the buzz of being busy. The kids raced throughout the day whilst Richard and I partook in stall business. My role was sales and setting up the stall and also keeping the day's takings safe. My husband was responsible for the fitting of products we were selling, and he also offered advice with regard to the products.

It was great teamwork. I loved the journey home, my husband driving along, two happy kids in the back seat with their shiny trophies in their young hands, and there I would be pulling out bank notes from every pocket. It was very satisfying to share these successful points in time on the journeys home. It was an overwhelming sense of achievement that we were sharing as a couple. These were really happy, fun weekends: kids winning races and enjoying the day with all their friends, being all together as a family and running a business that customers appreciated.

We then moved on to clothing printing. My husband and I still run the same business together to this day. We are a well-oiled machine. It's all down to teamwork. He does the artwork side of the business and I do the buying of the stock, printing logos onto the garments, organising quotes and arranging collections. We work like crazy idiots in the mornings so that, once lunchtime has passed, we have the afternoons free to enjoy what we love.

I have always loved baking, decorating, painting, sewing and going round charity shops. I suppose thinking about it now, sitting here writing, I didn't have many hobbies when I was a young mum. This year though has been my busiest, hobby-wise, I'm sure of it. I was trying to pack in as much as I could, you see, in case cancer took me!

When I decorate and the paint lid is off, I'm like a crazy, obsessed woman with a brush in my hand — everywhere is a danger! My family have to try and dodge all of the areas that are covered in fresh sticky paint! Once I start, I can't stop. I'm like a broken record, shouting "Watch that area, it's wet! Watch that area, I've painted there too!" My son often remarks at how mental I am once I get started on my painting frenzy.

My other loves are walking, riding my pushbike, walking my dog Tyla, going on my husband's motorbike, seeing my friends and being in my garden. There's nothing more peaceful than a sunny day surrounded by the beauty of the blooms, freshly cut grass and a cup of tea in the middle of the lawn sat at my brightly sprayed garden table. The chairs are metal, upcycled and now the colour of daffodil yellow. This is where I have sat and written some parts of this book.

Our village is so quiet. My garden offers sounds of the birds, bees and the planes flying overhead and sometimes the odd cow saying "moo" in the distance. What's not to love? Gardening though, is a very solitary hobby. This is something that I need to take note of now, and limit my time in the garden, giving me more time to enjoy other pleasures that you will soon read about.

When I Won The Jackpot

T his was the night of 24th February 1999. My friend Joanna and I were both hot to trot for a night in Nottingham, then off to a club called ISIS, which was the coolest place to dance.

We loved the pubs and clubs back then, and we were in our prime. I picked her up in my little blue Bedford Rascal florist van and into Nottingham we headed. I was driving and I didn't mind drinking soft drinks — I was looking for love!

The pubs were packed, the nightlife electric, the city was far from sleeping. This night would be the night that my fairy-tale started, but I did not know it yet. We bar-hopped and danced in many pubs. We wandered around Nottingham in the cold. We didn't need coats as we wanted to show off our outfits; we were young, stupid, and didn't feel the cold.

We visited the ladies toilets often to make ourselves look sexy and tip-top; I'm sure we would have had our midriffs out to gain as much attention as we could. I was out to impress! I was slim, sexy and confident. Joanna, I recall, had a steady boyfriend at the time — she is now married to him! Hi, Tony!

We had visited many pubs, and it was now time to drive to our favourite club, ISIS, where we planned to really let our hair down and dance the night away. I pulled up in the car park, my blue van chose a parking bay. Out we stepped to strut our stuff.

The best 90s disco music was filling our hearts with joy — songs so good that they still play to this day on the radio! Joanna and I lived for clubbing; we couldn't get enough of it. We had no cares, we still lived with our parents, and our wages were our own. We spent our money on clothes and going out every weekend. This was the life; we were carefree and clueless and had no idea of what adult life would offer up to us. We went to the club ISIS to dance on Friday, Saturday and Monday nights.

After we'd been there a few hours, my mate Joanna bumped into this lad that she knew. This was at the bar. He was a friend of hers and they were catching up. There I stood, feeling a bit of a lemon. Lots of males were walking past me, giving me the eye. The music was pumping and the evening was mighty fine.

Anyway, this bloke that Joanna was talking to at the bar had a mate with him. He was dashing, smelt good and was smartly dressed in a shirt and sexy tailored jeans. He had a smile that made me fancy the pants off him. He wasn't a nightclub knob head, I could tell; I knew instantly that he was a nice guy. His name was Richard.

Richard and I got chatting about how he was doing a house up and how he was ready to leave home and settle into this cottage he was telling me about. God, it seems like yesterday as I type this. Richard could have knocked me down with a feather. "I live in Ilkeston," he said, "with my mum and dad at the moment." I replied, "You're joking, I have a flower shop in Ilkeston on the high street!" We were both surprised that we were from the same area.

I was seeing a lad on and off at this point, but I said to Richard that I might seek him and his cottage out if this lad didn't work out!

Richard told me roughly where the village was, and then soon after this we parted ways and Joanna and I walked back to my van as the night was drawing to an end. Joanna asked, "How do you know that guy, then?" I replied, "I've only just met him tonight!" Joanna was shocked by this, as Richard and I had been getting on like a house on fire at the bar.

Richard was almost 27 when I met him, and I was a few weeks off turning 23. He had roughly explained to me where this house was that he was in the middle of renovating. So I'd replied, "I might visit you for a cuppa." This was when we were in our flirting stage at the bar.

Over the next few days, I couldn't stop thinking about Richard. I decided to dump the lad I was seeing and search for the man I'd met in ISIS. I wrote a brief letter with my phone number on it to jog his memory of our brief encounter.

I got all dolled up — best make-up, nice clothes and my favourite black faux fur coat. I climbed into my van, the most important letter I had composed in my entire life now placed on the passenger seat. Behind my seat were many flower deliveries of the day to drop off, but this letter was by far my most important delivery and my highest priority. Could I get this letter to its destination? To the man that was sending my heart crazy?

I drove down a narrow lane that Richard had described to me, following twisty roads, and then onto a tree-lined country road.

I reached a fork in the road and gave up — I couldn't see any cottages! "What the hell!" I thought. "He must have been giving me the brush off. He must have been telling me lies!"

I drove back up the lane. I was so sad. My heart was deflated; the plan hadn't unfolded as I had pictured it to. I reached the junction at the top of a road. I thought, "I should have driven a little bit further." So I turned my van back round and redid the journey, this time driving further than the fork in the road that I had originally given up at. I kept driving. "What's around this corner?" I thought. I spotted the cottages. "This is where my dream man comes to do up his house," I thought. My heart pounded. Was he going to be in when I knocked on his door?

No, he wasn't, so I pushed the note through the letterbox and had the longest afternoon and evening of my life as I waited for the call from my heart throb.

That night my phone finally rang! It was my Mr Gorgeous on the end of the line, saying, "When shall we go on a date then?"

We never announced that I was moving in — I just claimed a wardrobe! It all just unfolded so naturally. We got engaged in December 1999 and got married in August 2000. ISIS was that much of a special place to Richard and me that we even had our joint hen and stag do there! Our beautiful kids followed in March 2002 and July 2003. Our cottage and family were complete. This cottage has seen it all: our very beginning, the note though the letterbox, our growing, our getting engaged, walking over the threshold on the return from our honeymoon, and many years of excited faces at Christmas from Trin and Owen as they dashed down our stairs. Building our businesses, our babies growing into fine young adults, and now the latest milestone — a cancer battle.

Something so amazing came from tenacity and boldness — my perfect life. Aim high, because nothing is out if reach if you want it enough.

Spilling Oil

F riends, they were all part of my journey. Each one had no choice; every loyal friend I knew had to accept the black news. Their cases were already packed for the cancer journey ahead; they'd been chosen, even if they didn't want to travel with me. It was horrendous for everybody. Informing them of my uphill battle felt so cruel.

A few friends knew of my very few bleeds after intercourse; they'd thought that it was going to be something simple to sort, while I'd been on the fence. I had been researching, reading all the signs, and it pointed to cancer — my mind was accepting this a little more with each day that passed, from my bad bleed in May until the day in early July when I heard the doctor confirm that my worst fears were in fact a reality.

I returned home on receiving my news and, boom, it hit me. I was going to have to call my very dearest, oldest friends to inform them that my body was under attack and that I might die from this terrible disease. I slowly moved through my friends list, explaining what a dreadful mess I was in. It was a horrible task to follow through.

Friends were stunned. Each phone call ended with tears.

Shaking, crying, frightened voices said goodbye to me down the handset. Traysi, my friend of 30 years, was at work on an afternoon shift. She told me that she would come and get the news from me personally. She arrived at my house and sat on my living room sofa with a bundle of loo roll gripped tightly in her hand. "Go on then," she said, her fearful face looking straight at me. There it was — the moment I'd worry her stupid for a year or so. The words came spilling from my lips as I knelt down on my living room floor in front of my fire and told her how bad my health was.

Joanna was the next friend to tell; it was like a hit list. Horrible, shocking news to have to share with everyone I cared about. Joanna, remember, is my dear friend and former clubbing partner — my reason for meeting Richard. My eyes were like waterfalls. I felt sorry for everyone involved — myself, my family and friends.

Another dear friend of mine: Jenny; a friendship true and strong of 20 years. I now had to call her too and spread the black. I couldn't reach her; I called maybe seven times before she answered. Each unsuccessful call was so hard; I just wanted the terrible news off of my chest at least. Finally, I reached her at 8 p.m. I'd been dialling since about 4 p.m. I shared my news; she was devastated. She told me it would be a tough year ahead with a massive hill to climb but that I could beat this. Sobbing and low, I ended the call. I told her I loved her.

I dialled again; my friend Rachel. I waited for her to answer. "Hey ducky," Rachel's voice replied. "Terrible news," I said. "I've got cervical cancer." "Oh no!" she replied. I could hear her voice full of shock and dread. "My beautiful friends," I thought. "I hate doing these calls."

Off I went again, telling my friend Donna. I have known Donna since I was 20. Twenty-four years is a very long time to be friends. All of these friendships I'm mentioning are old, well-bonded and very special friendships. I knew Donna from my second job. We were in our early 20s when we were work pals; it was a fun time. We worked together every day for two years. The city of Nottingham was busy and alive, and we spent all our days together working and having a laugh. The market that we worked on in Victoria Centre was busy — full of hustle and bustle every day. It was a rich time in my life. They were wonderful carefree years when all I had to worry about was getting my pay packet and looking forward to spending it all at the weekend. The nightlife, going out, partying and getting chatted up were my only goals in life.

This was the moment, the very phone call, where I'd ruin her next 12 months or so. Her dear friend Michelle had cancer. Her voice was shaking with fear for me as we spoke about my diagnosis down the phone. People didn't know what to say to me. What can you say to terrible news like cancer? The phone call ended with her saying, "Love you, keep me posted." My eyes streamed with tears yet again. All of this was on 3rd July.

Little did I know, many more friends would willingly step up for me. These friends though were my keyboard friends as I have now named them, offering me laughs and light-hearted news of their days. As Covid-19 was here, friends could not visit me due to the restrictions. I was also having to be super careful as I was having chemotherapy, therefore making me immunocompromised. I did not want to catch illnesses from them and jeopardise my health even more. My immune system was taking a right battering from the chemotherapy. If I was to get an infection, then chemo treatment would have been postponed. Even worse, I could have ended up in hospital, where I could have been at increased risk of contracting Covid.

These lovely friends all kept me sane, and they all offered me happiness. Their names are Martina, Mandy, Diane Wright, Andy W and all my village neighbours. All these folk really stepped up for me and these friendships grew stronger. All these wonderful people will say that they didn't do anything special, but they offered me distraction and love, which were worth their weight in gold. Light-hearted messages that kept my brain from thinking about cancer; messages that would land in front of my eyes when the TV was terrible; messages that I'd receive as the quiet evenings would draw in, the time when dark thoughts would circle my brain if I wasn't busy thinking of other things.

These messages kept me mentally sound, so thank you one and all. The keyboard messages stopped the cloak of cancer from covering my personality and mind. All the messaging and friendships and upbeat family life were the key. This kept me happy, focussed, busy, feeling loved, not feeling alone. It made the days easier to cope with. The time passed much quicker when I had keyboard chats with new friends. It meant cancer couldn't smother my personality. All my family and friends have served me so well; I can never repay you all.

Each day was glorious getting to know my village neighbours; they were and still are great friends to me, and just a hop, skip and jump away from my front door. This again was, and is, something so priceless that I hold so dear to my heart.

So here it was, the day that I shared my news with neighbours. We live in a small hamlet, and I was not going to be able to hide my bald head whilst walking my dog on our village green. I also realised that people would spot my massive bow when I was driving out of the village, so therefore I told most neighbours my grim diagnosis.

The bow on my head was an idea of mine from the very start, when I was told I would lose my hair. I decided a huge floral bow would be my way of loving losing the hair and embracing cancer. I was determined to be out and about in my village and our local fields as much as I could; I was going to carry on as normal and look stunning doing so. To be honest, I was looking forward to wearing a massive bow on my head. I practised the bow to perfection most nights at my bedroom mirror, ready, prepared and waiting for the day that my hair of 44 years received its curtain call.

I walked, filled with sadness, to neighbours' houses that I was closest to. These had been my neighbours for 20 years plus. Some of them in the village were not that close, but Covid-19 would bring us closer together as a village in the months to come. My neighbours were stunned at what I had to tell. A beautiful summer's day with the darkest of news. I looked so well and healthy; nobody found the news easy to accept.

After sharing with them what was to come for me in the months ahead, I walked back down to my house feeling low and robbed of my health. I might be embarking on a downward spiral towards death, I feared.

The next blow was on 11th July, two days after hearing my diagnosis. The sun was shining and the grass was growing at such a fast pace. I was looking out of my bedroom window and all I could think to myself was that I couldn't be bothered to keep it neat and tidy; the depression of ill health had taken my spark away. I love gardening, you see. I had been a very keen gardener for the previous five years, but the cancer arrived and as quick as a flash, my passion for gardening was no more. The desire to spend time with my love, my garden, had absolutely vanished. I had to force myself to mow the lawn and do a few tidying-up jobs. Walking around my beautiful garden in early July offered me no joy whatsoever. I have a friend who loves to care for her garden. Her name is Diane Wright. I phoned Diane and offered her about twenty baby delphinium plants as I'd grown them from seed and they were all over my garden in pots. The desire to love and look after them all was now non-existent; twenty-odd thriving delphiniums sat needing care and I couldn't be bothered to nurture them.

My friend didn't accept. She did me a huge favour though, as I now had to tend to them. The plants hung on in there with the minimum care that I could just about muster, and lived through the summer months. Thank you, Diane, I owe you a few delphiniums. You pushed me into having to look after the young plants, and this gave me purpose.

As gardening had been my hobby for the past five years, my body was a slim size 8 and in tip-top condition — ha, apart from cancer that is. The digging, mowing, weeding and walking up and down the garden path to water my many plants had stood me in good stead. My garden had made my body super healthy, other than the cancer which was dividing and taking refuge in my blood stream, pelvic area and lymph node. I'd been totally unaware of my disease.

The whole summer of 2020 was missed; I was either in hospital having treatment or at home with no enthusiasm for my beautiful love: my garden. The blooms were showing me their love, but I had nothing to give back: cancer had snatched away my pizazz.

My really sad period lasted a good few weeks, until week 3 came along and then my life changed forever. You will soon come to this chapter.

Beautiful Friendships

I have known Mandy for about six years. But this one year from 2020 to 2021 would really show me how supportive she was willing to be. She and her husband Lee, good family friends of ours, popped to see Richard and I at distance. I was receiving chemotherapy at the time and was told to mix with as few people as possible in case I caught viruses. It was hard telling them what may lie ahead for our close-knit family. They were stunned and upset. Off they went back to their hometown of Carlton, rocked by what we had revealed to them.

Soon after this, our Messenger messages picked up pace. We didn't realise it then, but this was going to be a deep and true typing friendship. Mandy and I shared a jovial humour. Many of my other friends are also "glass half-full" people and my Mandy was no different. We would build on our friendship over the nine months, her joking about her "wrap-around dress" that she wore all the time due to her working from home because of Covid. Her wrap-around dress was her dressing gown. Mandy, such a cheerful, delicate, slim-built lady with a beautiful giggle and smile. Her fine blonde hair gives her the look of a Christmas angel you'd place on your tree each year.

Mandy would joke about her other dresses not zipping up because she'd driven too many chocolate eggs into her face! She would lift my spirits with every message received. What a true friend. Mandy, you are an angel. One of my keyboard angels when we couldn't have a coffee together.

I have already mentioned Traysi briefly. We met when I was only 16 years of age at my first ever job. We go back a long way, and I can't believe that she is still in my life. I am now 45! We did have a gap of not knowing where each other was for about 10 years. Life just got in the way. Then I went shopping in Nottingham with my husband one weekday, and someone shouted, "Little Michelle!" It was Traysi shouting me. Traysi is like a big sister to me, with all the qualities you desire in a sister and no faults whatsoever. She was shell-shocked to hear of my diagnosis. She brought me flowers all through my cancer journey just to try and cheer me up and show how much she cared.

Love you, Traysi. You are another angel on my journey. Your strength and friendship are so dear to me. Traysi would message me every Tuesday when I had chemotherapy treatment days. I would be sitting there waiting to be called by a nurse and my mobile phone would ping. It would be Traysi. The message would say "Hope chemo goes well", or something like that. It was as if she was bloody psychic. Her heart of gold has helped me through my darkest times.

Traysi, you are like my mum and sister all rolled into one. What a fabulous friend you are. Thank you for the hundreds of messages we're shared throughout my journey; I am forever in your debt.

What a pal. You sweet angel of mine.

Jenny is my next dear loyal friend. Jenny has beautiful long, thick, brown hair. When she walks towards me, her mass of shiny, bouncy, layered, healthy hair bobs up and down. I am greeted with her massive happy smile. She always has such a warming aura. She is always so helpful and friendly to everyone who demands her time, to the point that she has no quality time for herself. She is a people-pleaser. She does a lot for her local church.

I've known Jenny 18 years. I met Jenny at a playgroup when my two children were very tiny tots. Jenny is strong, reliable, and always there for me. She has a massive fluffy heart filled with pink candy-floss-coloured feathers.

Jenny, I am adding this story to this book because the memories of our recent holiday now sit deep in my heart. The camping trip in August 2021 was great fun and offered plenty of memory-making, which I will hold dear forever. Spending three whole days with you — instead of having you for a few hours, which is what usually happens when we meet for a chat — is something that I found so precious. Saying goodnight to you and eating our breakfast together were a true delight and honour.

I loved washing the pots with you, and the memories of the fairy light treasure hunt around the campsite are deep within my heart. What a friend you have been to me for so many years. Here's to 18 more, hopefully setting up camp together in every year that follows.

Okay, so I've briefly mentioned Joanna already. She was my partner in crime the night that Richard stole my heart! She is calm, reserved, sensible, very grounded, and always smartly dressed. She is an old school friend; we go back a long way and I have known her since I was 17. It broke my heart to tell her I was unwell, as it did with all my friends. We were clubbing friends and we also did a car share because we both worked in Nottingham town centre in our twenties. This happened every day for a good few years.

She was a travel agent, and I was a florist. The car sharing was such a laugh! We built our bond on these many car journeys, didn't we, Jo? Two young females in our prime and we knew it — no cares in the world apart from boys and friendships. Joanna and I would carpool at weekends too. I would drive when we went drinking and clubbing in Nottingham. I would be on soft drinks of course, but I would collect her in my car from her mum and dad's house. Joanna would dash out all dolled up, looking dressed to kill, climb in my car, give me an excited smile and flip down the visor vanity mirror to improve her make-up. God, Jo, these are such beautiful memories of mine and I know they are yours too.

I lost touch with Joanna at the age of 26 — getting married, becoming a mum and general life just came between our friendship. Joanna's life took the same path as mine. I hit 29 and missed her terribly so decided to do some digging. I wrote a letter and posted it to her parents' house, the house that I used to collect Joanna from when we shared our girlie drinking nights out. I pulled out the home phonebook and looked for her maiden surname and spotted her mum and dad's Hucknall address. Only you more mature readers will relate to a phonebook, ha-ha! This was a long shot but my only lead to search for my lost friend who had moulded my early life so much.

To my delight, she wrote back to me — she had received my letter. Her family had passed the letter along a chain of family members. This glittering day is so vivid in my memory. This was in 2005, 16 years ago. There I was with a brush in my hand, sweeping away leaves from my driveway. I must have been decorating that day too as I also remember that I was wearing my cream painting dungarees. Richard walked towards me with an envelope in his hand and said, "You have a letter, buddy!" My heart began to pound. I hoped it would be from my dear Joanna. You didn't fail me then and you haven't failed me through my fight either. Now go and dry your face!

Here follows how our friendship came about. What loyal friends we became, the night you joined me and some other girls for a drink in Nottingham! Joanna and I have a mutual friend called Rhonda. She is to thank for our timeless friendship. Rhonda, you are a total star. Rhonda invited Joanna along to come and join us for drinks round Nottingham one night. That is 28 years ago now. You became my everything from that moment forward: my friend, my front seat passenger, the one I shared stories of my shitty workdays with as we travelled home to Hucknall. You were the friend I couldn't wait to pick up and start my weekends with. Joanna, this chapter has made my eyes fill. What a beautiful past we have built.

What a fantastic night that was, and your gutsy spirit created a friendship above and beyond my wildest dreams. Your decision that night has impacted my life — impacted my heart.

Life in 2012 was very busy for us both. Jo became a mum for the third time and gave birth to her daughter Phoebe. Richard and I were busy building our business at the BMX shop along with Trinity and Owen racing every weekend. The friendship was neglected and led to us drifting apart. Now we didn't have much of a clue about each other's lives. In 2019 though, Trin and I nipped to Ilkeston Argos to look for a Christmas gift for my son. There we stood, flicking through the Argos catalogue that was on display, when I heard this voice say, "Hey, Michelle!" It was my dear wonderful lost friend standing opposite me. Oh my God, I was so pleased to catch up with her! We agreed to look each other up on Facebook.

Our friendship has been wonderful from that day forwards. Joanna sent me some beautiful earrings through the post when I told her of my news. They are called friendship knots. They arrived in a sweet little silver tin with my name inside it. How thoughtful of her. My darling friend Joanna, another angel of mine. Flipping heck, I love you.

Rachel. She is valued highly in my friends list too. I met her at 21 years of age when I went on holiday. We were great friends from 21 to 26 but then we lost touch as she went travelling and I was well into my chapter of being a wife and mum of two beautiful little sausages, my children, Trin and Owen. It was so many years that passed, and I just didn't know how to find her. I looked on Facebook but couldn't recall her surname.

At the end of 2016, Christmas decorations were needed from the loft. There sat my box of wedding keepsakes next to the items I was up there for. My brain chose to go down memory lane and look through the box. I pulled out my tiara, my shoes, all sorts of beautiful memories and then, to my beating heart's joy, there it was: a seating plan of our wedding day meal scribbled on a piece of paper, showing about 50 guests. There she sat, Rachel Herbert. Oh, the happiness! My heart raced. This could be it — could I find her now? I quickly vacated the loft, dashed downstairs and jumped onto my phone and onto Facebook. Worried she might now have changed her maiden name, I was crossing every bone in my body, so longing to find my dear friend.

She was so dear, in fact, that on my wedding day, she and her then boyfriend decorated our evening venue for us. I trusted her implicitly to do a fabulous job. I was a florist at the time, and quite a control freak, wanting things done to perfection. I suppose a bridezilla actually! Her and her then squeeze blew up about 300 helium balloons for me. When we got to the venue that afternoon, these 300-odd balloons danced on the back of guests' chairs and in the middles of many tables. Big foil hearts and also standard balloons floated in the air; they gave the huge reception room depth and amazement. All her doing, all her hard work and all her love for me was on display. Thank you, my dear friend.

Anyway, yes, I found her on Facebook. I messaged her, and she answered me straight away. I had found my long-lost diamond ring. Then my phone rang. I picked up. "Hey ducky," she said, and the years we'd been apart seemed like a speck of dust — it was brilliant. We are great friends still, and I won't be letting her fly away ever again. I need to keep this balloon tied to my wrist. My beautiful Rachel.

Now here is a friendship that came out of nowhere. Emily is 31 and such a lovely young lady — caring, big-hearted and always smiling. She is brave but doesn't realise it. She has a toddler, Arthur, who melts all of the neighbours' hearts. She brings him into the village to splash in puddles and find sticks. He's yummy — his blonde hair and cute face would melt an iron heart. He can now blow the neighbours a kiss. He wanders round like an old man with his hands behind his back. Hello Arthur, here is your moment of fame — at such a young age!

At Christmas, mine and Emily's friendship was just unfolding as we got to know each other's little quirks; each other's loveable characters. It was like a snowball being rolled along the ground, starting off small but turning into something to be proud of.

I'm glad we weren't this close though when I was receiving treatment as I think she would have worried too much about my diagnosis; I think it would have been very upsetting for her. Emily offered giggles and fun when I needed to make the waiting for treatment news pass by quicker. She is such a brilliant neighbour and friend and just on my doorstep about 100 yards away. Emily was very fearful on 16th March 2021, the day that I received my final news.

Oh, my dear friend Emma. Now here is a truly happy story. Emma, along with my family and one other friend Martina, really made my cancer journey truly golden. This sounds so bonkers, having cancer and experiencing a golden year, but that's a spot-on evaluation of how I view my journey. I realise wholeheartedly now that I am a people person — I adore friendship. Who doesn't?

Having the right friends around you, as I have so recently experienced, can pull you through any nightmare. Brilliant family and friends make for a very enriched existence, I believe. My family, whom I so truly adore, are the purest gold of all. How lucky I am to have such a humongous support wrapped around me.

Emma was a neighbour of 20 years. Before Covid-19 and cancer came along, we would only smile and wave when seeing each other out in the village. I often saw her walking with a book in her hand, and I thought this was bizarre — how could she possibly be engrossed in any book and not trip over whilst walking along? Looking down at her book, moving forwards to her destination of choice whilst soaking up a riveting plot.

On 11th July I knocked on Emma's door and told her of my journey ahead. "Oh no!" she said. "Well, if you ever fancy a walk or coffee, you know where I am." We were about three months into Covid-19 restrictions by now, so all the village seemed to lean on each other that little bit more.

I decided to take Emma up on her offer and we soon embarked on our new friendship. I wasn't a huge walking enthusiast, but Emma could rack up the miles like a bee collecting pollen; she could just go and go. Our first walk was a tough learning curve for me; my shins were killing me. We covered about 6 miles, and my shins were in A&E on returning home. I had decided, you see, to do our first ever walk in wellies, and my ankles were throbbing like mad. Wellies offered me very little support. Soon after this, I purchased better footwear to walk in, as the fields were getting muddy.

The walking and talking was wonderful — it was invaluable to offload my fears. Friendship was unfolding every day that we walked. Laughing and bonding, our relationship grew much stronger; every walk I did with her, I loved her so much more. Emma was my sunshine even on a windy Autumn day. We began walking in the month of July 2020 when we were blessed with beautiful sunny days, and then we walked through August to December, experiencing all of the season's changes.

Now it was cold and muddy on our walks, but on we charged, sticking to our daily meets. Most days we walked, and every day we WhatsApped. It was blissful; my heart was filled with joy due to her presence in my life. She was the flake in my 99 ice cream. We were the walking queens of the village. We were both less busy at work due to lockdown, and we abused every minute of our spare time. We loved walking and giggling; the conversation always flowed so easily.

On the walks we would bring cut-up fruit or apples in our pockets. We would walk to local beauty spots and woods and soak up the views of the seasonal changes nature was in charge of. It was an intense friendship. Cancer and Covid had been the root of it evolving, but I loved every minute of being with Emma and her big heart.

God, she knew such personal things about me. I would get phone calls from hospital about medical matters that worried me, and she would be within earshot of my questions and answers down my handset. On a few occasions, she was in stitches at the conversation I was having with the nurse on my mobile phone as we walked along; they were very personal female matters that she was within earshot of. This didn't worry me in the slightest though, as we had come to a stage of our friendship where there was no embarrassment, only fun and love.

It truly was like having a sister on my doorstep. It was amazing, as my own sister lives a two-hour journey away. We shared so many hobbies; this was soon very apparent. We loved the simple things in life: cooking, baking, gardening and crafting. We loved nature and we hated waste.

At Christmas time, at the beginning of December 2020, we decided to do a lot of dark evening walks. Over fields we'd walk, our aim being to find pretty houses laden with fairy lights — we both loved a good showy house, dancing with colour. We spotted reindeer lit up, huge trees with coloured bulbs all over them, trees that had no life to them but that were covered with confetti of the soft creamy twinkly spots adorning them. What a delight!

It was freezing but memorable; these special images are imprinted in my mind forever. Even writing this now, in March 2021, it's something that makes my heart skip, to revert back to seeing all those pretty images with my dear faithful friend.

Emma loved making her own liquor. She would bring this, and I would load up my coat pockets with Quality Street sweets. What the hell, I thought, it was Christmas after all! A great combination when walking in the dark. Our breath would create mist in the air, it was that cold. We would walk so far, to a particularly well-trimmed house, and get these little old-fashioned shot glasses out of our pockets, fill them with her homemade fruity liquor and say "Cheers!" We'd walk along sipping fruity vodka followed by sweet chocolates whilst soaking up the coloured twinkly lights that trimmed people's gardens and properties. It was magical.

We would have our knitted gloves wrapped around these tiny glasses. There was nobody about, only us lapping up the beauty of Christmas fairy light displays. The streets empty, all humanity were safe and sound inside their warm, cosy living rooms with their central heating on. But my special friend Emma and I were out soaking up the joy of Christmas spirit; it was like a VIP viewing as we walked along. She has carried on being a wonderful friend. I'm so grateful I have found her. I'm so appreciative of her friendship. Emma, you are beautiful.

Diana and I started to grow our friendship in late December. She is another neighbour that lives in my village, and it soon became apparent to me how much I valued her company. By the time my birthday arrived on 3rd March 2021 she was very dear to me, a real good soul that I could depend on.

Diana has beautiful, platinum blonde, shoulder-length hair. She has an infectious dirty laugh and is always jolly, always upbeat; she is a tonic to be with. She's a bit of a mummy figure to me — not in an old way, but in a caring way. She is in the same pretty box as Traysi: like a really mature older sister, maybe that's the best way that I view her. She's always such fun and so easy to get on with. I'll let you into a thought that I have, and that is that Diana looks very much like my wonderful mam. The likeness in their features and character warms my heart.

So, if you've been paying attention through the book, you'll know that I'm super lucky as I have found three really wonderful female neighbours that are brilliant friends, all on my doorstep, and this is all down to Covid-19 and cancer. We've become such a nice little group within one year: me, Emma, Emily and Diana. I love spending time with these fab three and they have made my journey very rich indeed.

A funny story about Diana that I have to share is this: I loved it on my birthday when I noticed you walking down to my porch. In a gift bag that Diana handed me was a bright yellow primrose plant, and I will never forget how you said it was the hardest thing you had ever had to wrap up, showering me with your cheeky, dirty laugh as you shared your story of the wrapping difficulty. To explain to you readers, the plant was in a metal watering can and an impossible shape to manoeuvre around. That still makes me smile as I type your comment, Diana. My 45th birthday was so very special — all three of you neighbours made such a fuss of me. On this date, my birthday, I only had 13 days' wait ahead to see if I was out of the woods as my MRI result day was creeping up fast.

Diane Wright is another lovely friend. She has such a giving heart, is very bubbly and is a tonic to be with. Diane is a friend of 11 years. She loves plants and gets totally lost in my back garden when it's in full bloom. She even says that my garden in past years has encouraged her to add more colour to *her* garden. I am flattered, Diane!

Diane popped for a cuppa today. Behind where we sat this afternoon is a massive flower bed. It is abundant with cosmos, cornflowers and white huge daisies; it looked a picture. Diane is the friend I asked to collect the baby delphinium plants from my house in the first few weeks after my diagnosis when I had lost my spark for my beautiful garden, back in July 2020. She declined, do you recall?

Because Diane wouldn't accept these plants, she did me a huge favour. I had no choice but to drag my sorry arse into the garden and keep all twenty alive. Today they waved hello as we sat and drank our tea on the lawn, having a right good catch-up. We revelled in each other's company as it had been so many months since we'd physically sat together due to Covid restrictions. Today Diane took home a huge purple delphinium plant, a gift I handed to her to say thank you for giving me purpose through those very black weeks.

I'm going to add this story in because it warrants great recognition. My daughter and I went to watch an outdoor cinema film at a beautiful local park in August 2021, and I really wanted to replicate the event in my village. My neighbour Janet offered for me to hold this event on her massive front lawn. Janet, you are a star. Twenty-five friends sat and enjoyed a well-known musical. It was a great success!

I named my party event "Big cinema night". Diane came up with the genius idea of doing a raffle for Cancer Research. Diane, it was so thoughtful of you and made the film night such fun, as we drew the raffle on the same evening before the film started. Our night raised £648.50 from raffle ticket sales, printed t-shirts and popcorn cones. Diane and I had to hand-write 2,500 names on separate raffle tickets between us both, which was a hellish task. Individually, each tiny ticket — all 2,500 of the devils — had to be folded, which was also something that gives me nightmares!

Diane and I laughed so much about this. What great teamwork, but all Diane's idea, and Diane gathered many wonderful raffle prizes too. Diane, I loved being your plus-one on this occasion.

The Beast

O n receiving the cancer news, I was absolutely terrified; it was very daunting. My husband tried to do everything to lift my mood. He informed me that he had spotted a car I would love. I was disheartened and low and wasn't keen on driving out to view cars, but I thought, "Oh well, it will give me some fresh air to take a trip out and look through some car windows." The dealership was about a five-minute drive away. Off we went with no clue that this day was going to be the day when I waved goodbye to a large chunk of our ISA savings!

We arrived at the forecourt of the local car dealers in Ilkeston. My husband Richard pointed to the car he had seen for me as our vehicle came to a standstill in the customer parking bays. Wow, it was stunning! The car that he had spotted for me was amazing. As my eyes saw the vehicle, I thought to myself, "Oh my God, that's way too posh for me to drive around in!"

There on the forecourt it sat, a bright blue Honda Civic EX, its £13,800 price tag hung in the windscreen. It was a huge, five-door lump of sexiness, parked there showing off its demeanour, knowing it was top dog of the selection of cars that were on display. It really did speak to my heart. "Come and look at me," the car said. "You know you want me," this bright blue spaceship whispered. It beckoned my sad heart. The price big, bold and way out of my budget. Or so I told myself.

The youngest car I would ever buy. The most expensive car I would ever buy. Most definitely the sexiest car I would ever buy. "The last car I might ever buy!" I thought. "I must buy it because this could be my only chance to ever own a sports car!" This is what was running through my mind as I walked towards it, peering inside the blacked-out windows as I gave in to its invitation to enjoy it.

So, I'd seen the car on the forecourt. It was stunning, it was a beast, its bonnet growled at me, its bodywork was strong and mean. It was a bloody wide car; its wheel arches were really flared, which gave it a mean sporty look. Its blue paintwork glistened as the sun caught the glitter within the paint mix. Its wing mirrors were spaceship-like. Its leather seats drew my eyes into the dash area of the car. As I looked, as I moved around the car, my mind and eyes enjoyed every inch of this vehicle. I was saying to my husband, "Oh I love it! Look at it! It's too much money though. It's £13,800, for God's sake!"

My husband replied, "Just test-drive it. You don't have to buy it!" "Okay," I replied. I was naïve and stupid; my bank balance went down near on £14,000 right there and then as I got my husband to nip inside and tell the kind salesman that his wife would like to test-drive the Honda parked outside on the forecourt. I took the keys from the salesman. I opened the car door and sat in this dazzling car. I touched the sporty steering wheel and couldn't wait for my test drive to unfold; it was the kind of car that anybody's heart would have fallen for. You would have to have had a heart of stone to resist its sex appeal!

It's like saying to a child, "Put your hands in this jar of sweets but don't take any." I was the child that day, reaching down into the jar; wasn't I a massive idiot thinking it wouldn't steal my heart! I climbed in. Wow, the interior smelt lush. A freshly valeted fragrance hit my nostrils, and the leather bucket seats made my mind happy. I took it for a test drive.

I looked at the bonnet through the windscreen; it looked like Batman's car. The bonnet's flared shape was dominating; it was wider than that of my little sporty-looking vehicle. But the real difference was that my little white car told passers-by something that it was not: it looked fast, but it wasn't!

This beauty I was now sitting in was mean, wide and beefy. My heart raced; I wanted to eat up miles in this car. It had bags of style and elegance, and oozed prowess — everything the boy racer in me longed for. The car meant business as it tempted my right foot with its turbo engine. It offered up 128 bhp — more than the vehicle that I was driving around at the time, much more.

The dark grey smoke alloy wheels gave the Honda a very stylish look too. The tinted blacked-out windows were lovely. There was nothing could I fault. I pulled off the forecourt and onto the main road; my test drive began to unfold. The beast was grown up, it was wide, it was powerful. It had buckets of growl and attitude, and I loved it. I started to move through the gears — God, it was responsive! I was amazed! I was excited! Conscious that I was driving in a 40 mph zone, I drove very steadily and was super careful with this very expensive chunk of luxury. I couldn't wait to hit the 60 mph zone to give it some welly and let the turbo show me what I was missing out on.

The car was perfection, peaceful and what I desired. There it was, the national speed limit sign. This was the moment that my foot fell in love with the turbo of this sexy beast. It went like stink! It made me smile; it made me say "Oh my God" out loud. The turbo joined us around the bends as I squeezed my right foot to the floor, the leather padded bucket seats holding me tight like a giant. The grunt of the turbo could be heard inside the car — it was fantastic, nothing could I fault. I had the biggest smile on my face; I was falling in love right there and then. "I want it," I thought. "I deserve it," I thought.

I returned back from the test drive and played it cool. An hour later, after wandering around my house trying to tell my heart I could not purchase it, I caved in and left a deposit by phone as I could not stop thinking about how beautiful it was. That was it, you see — it had stolen my heart on the very short ten-minute test drive that I had experienced. It had plucked a piece of my heart out as I handed back the key fob. Like the car in the film "Christine", it wanted me.

The love story began, and three days later the car was on my drive. Every morning when I opened my living room curtains, I couldn't believe it was mine. My next-door neighbour commented, "Wow, beautiful car, Michelle!" This is when I told her that I had cancer and that I had treated myself. She looked at me tearfully and was stunned. She had been out that day when I had informed most village neighbours of my news.

My love drove me to hospital and back home every day. Me and my beast, travelling to save my life. It offered me fun, loud music, power and friendship. Its dashboard witnessed all of my worry, fear and anxiousness to be me again — to be healthy. The seats hugged me tightly when I couldn't control my sadness. It was my thrill; it was my chauffeur to chemo and radiotherapy. My huge blue sporty friend.

When I was overwhelmed, it got me home safely. It was and is my gentle giant. Stupid, I know, but it's another beautiful friend that I so very much appreciated on my journey. I used to arrive at the hospital car park and pray that there would be a huge end spot somewhere out of the way, so that my precious friend wouldn't get its doors bumped by some ignoramus!

It made my terrifying trips to the hospital fun ones. There I would sit, lapping up its power and prowess as I did the 30-mile round trip. Twice a week for six weeks to start with, as blood samples were on a Monday and chemo then followed on the Tuesday. After six weeks of this treatment plan and putting many unwanted miles on my speedometer, my sexy beast was then a very busy fellow, as I then had to attend hospital every day for five weeks — I was now having radiotherapy every day to my pelvic area for the cervical cancer. My body was now getting a thrashing from radiation.

Every day my beast did not fail me; every day it looked after me. As soon as it saw tears drop into my lap it quickly said, "Here, use my turbo as your tissue, Michelle." I would accept its kind gesture along the country roads there and back from Derby to Ilkeston. Every mile was so much fun and total indulgence. The drive gave the distance and treatment a different purpose; it was a journey where I could play on the tarmac and push this top-dollar toy to its limits.

I look out of the window now, a year on from it becoming a family member, a year on from it being my pride and joy, and I still think it is as sexy as the day I clapped eyes on it.

I wash it quite often, as I hate to spoil its beauty with the muck that our country lane offers up, and when the farmer has been muck spreading I drive like a granny. I think to myself and also say out loud, "Bloody road, it's going to ruin my beautiful clean car." I think, as I drive along the lane, "I'm sorry you're getting splattered in cow crap, my darling."

My husband thinks I have a screw loose! He often remarks, "Why are you driving this slowly? Speed up!" I reply, "No, I'm not getting my car dirty!" I just want to look after it so brilliantly, just as it has looked after me. It has given me top care and respect and has played a massive part in the scariest year that I have experienced. You are my blue sparkly angel and I love you dearly. It might have been a lot of money to shell out on myself, but every mile that I clocked up in my love to accept the punishment my treatment was inflicting on my body took the emphasis off the terrible chances of how my future might unfold.

It could never know how it has impacted on my heart, but it's been such a super friend to me. I will never forget my wonderful beast. I am forever in its debt for lifting my crushed heart of 2020. When I read this story for errors, tears flow as it has kept my heart from falling to bits.

Chemo Loneliness

On Monday 13th July I had to go into hospital and learn about chemotherapy. The Friday before this, I'd been told my cancer was very advanced. My world had been turned upside down. At this point, I was just in total shock; stuff was happening at such a fast rate. My appointment was at 11 a.m. at the Royal Derby Hospital; I thought this was for chemotherapy information and a brief chat. I was informed after sitting on the chair only a few minutes that I was scheduled for treatment the very next day!

"Okay Michelle," a very kind nurse said, "We have you booked in for tomorrow's chemotherapy." I was totally gobsmacked; I was astounded. I was literally coming back the next day for chemo; it was totally bewildering. I was delighted though that medical intervention was on the cards for the very next day.

The nurse stated that I would be clinically vulnerable; I would have to carry an emergency card in case I got sepsis, which can be life threatening to chemo patients. Bloody hell, it was frightening, and a lot to take in. A different nurse weighed me, took my bloods, and gave me tons of leaflets to read, ready for the next day's visit when I would truly be able to call myself a cancer patient as I would be sitting in the chemotherapy ward. I was given a tour of the chemotherapy bays — the look of them as I stood there petrified me. I saw many patients who were in the same boat as me. I thought, "This can't be happening to me!" It was absolutely terrifying.

Can you imagine, all this information and witnessing these scary sights, then thinking, "That is what my life is going to amount to tomorrow!" My brain was saying, "No, you aren't this poorly!" It was heart-crushing. I felt as fit as a fiddle and looked it too.

Everything was daunting — the severity, the beeping machines, the seriousness of it all. I just couldn't believe that this is what my life had come to. I drove home in disbelief that this was going to be my next chapter. It was nuts. I was over the moon though, that treatment was the next day. But I had to get used to the idea of receiving chemotherapy so quickly. I'm truly grateful that it was so swift; it was a massive wake-up call as to how worried the hospital were about my health and how bad a state I was in.

Treatment days would come round so fast. Chemo days were the first treatments I experienced. I feared them; I didn't know what to expect. I would be thinking, take snacks, leave on time, can I get a parking space? Take activities to while away the many hours that I knew I would have to sit in the chemo chair for. Is my phone charged? Have I got my headphones? Have I got all the relevant paperwork? Do I need to put fuel in my car? Have I got my mask, my tablet and anything I need to help the day seem more enjoyable and less arduous?

I'd be planning the night before what clothing to wear. The chemo drip makes going to the toilet very tricky. If I wore something like an all-in-one jumpsuit then I wouldn't be able to get my arm through the armhole as the thin pipe that had the chemo was feeding into my hand and would mean that I couldn't pull a summer all-in-one suit down. Ha, it took a lot of planning to get the day to run smoothly. Pulling up tight trousers really pulled on the cannula that was inserted into the vein on the top of my hand. If I forgot and wore certain trousers that were tight-fitting round the waist, then I would pay dearly in pain as I pulled up my trousers.

The second rounds of chemo were very unkind to my kidneys, so the nurses on the chemo ward had to keep an eye on how much fluid I was urinating out. I was given a grey cardboard-like potty that I had to place on top of the toilet seat and wee into; this was so that the nurses could measure my urine and make sure that my body was flushing away the chemo safely through my kidneys. It was very undignified, but it had to be done to make sure my body was coping with the chemo poison. Each time I went for a wee, I would return to my chair and have to inform a nurse that my potty was waiting for them to take a fluid measurement from. Aren't nurses angels, the daily jobs they are faced with! We really don't have a clue. This more potent chemo was the cause of me having to drink more fluids so as to keep my bladder flushing away the bad. It was a vicious circle — I would drink more so that my body's organs weren't being harmed, but this made my day even trickier because I had to keep making toilet trips.

There was too much time on my hands on the chemo days to sit and reflect at what a state I was in. This cancer could take me, I used to sit and think. These could be the last months I have, and I was using my precious time sitting with chemo dripping into my hand at the speed of a tortoise walking along. I would sit there and think, "I'm bored, I want to go home. I want to be with my family — not doing this." I would look at the blue skies of summer through the hospital windows and want to walk out in protest. I didn't want the clinical hospital chair to be my weekly keeper, I just wanted my freedom and health back.

I turned up at the ward on the first Tuesday of chemotherapy feeling as bright as a button, as bright as I am now. I arrived at the chemo bay that a nurse had led me to, looked forward and thought, "I don't want to be part of this! Is this really happening to me?" My mind and bottom having to surrender to one of the chairs that waited for my suffering body. Every week I would choose a chair; it was soul destroying. It was with a heavy heart that I would get settled in for the whole day — six hours of treatment. Sitting in my chair of choice to take my medication to punish the cancer, there were many patients all around me in the bays. Many of them were sleeping though, and this made it a very lonely six hours as I had nobody to communicate with. The nurses made conversation whenever they came to sort out the packs of liquid chemo that hung on the stand that I could wheel along to the toilet. The amazing nurses that cared for me were wonderfully friendly but run off their feet.

Many patients around me were nodding or reading their books. I would have liked to engage in conversation, but they were not my age group. They'd be staring down at their books, or their eyelids would be closed tight sleeping. Every patient on every Tuesday was older than me.

I could not sleep; I had too much to do, in my mind at least. I couldn't rest; my mind didn't give in to the slow pace of a chemo day. I took tasks with me to show that I had made the most of sitting there for all those many hours. I'd write letters to my friends or my daughter Trinity. I even did business — end-of-year book work. Thank God for my keyboard friends. "Keyboard" — an amusing word. It means keys on a board, but I think of the word as keys so I wasn't bored through the day. The time on the ward would drag. The hands on the clock would sometimes, I felt, not move one single stroke. I would often think, "Have the flipping batteries run out in that damn thing?" But no, they were just very slow, boring days.

My hospital trolley was always covered in crap, ha-ha! Books, phone, colouring pencils, colouring book, writing paper, headphones, snacks, handbag, cross stitch — it was all on there; my trolley looked so funny compared to every other patient's trolley. There was no bloody room for my lunch when it arrived. I would have to apologise and clear away my many items for the day's distractions. One day I took pistachio nuts as my snack. When I stood up to go for one of my many toilet visits, there were hard shells all over the shop! All over the chair that I had been sitting in, all over my lap; some shells had escaped and got trapped in the crease of the seat, where my bottom had rested for so long. I apologised for being so messy, and the nurses laughed at me.

There was no nicer, sweeter sound to my ears than the nurse saying, "Right Michelle, you're done — you're free to go." God, that feeling of being released was as sweet as candy. I couldn't pack away my bag of distractions fast enough — I was out of there like a whippet on a racetrack. Into the sunny afternoon I would step and think, "God, I've missed another beautiful Tuesday." I would walk across the car park and happily climb into my beast, my blue sporty friend. Richard would collect me as I'd feel drained from the long days.

As we travelled home, I knew it wouldn't be long before I was fast asleep. I was always so drained from the long steady day. After I'd returned home and eaten the cooked dinner that Richard always made before fetching me, I wouldn't be able to keep my eyes awake any longer due to this terrible torture — chemotherapy.

As soon as I'd had my teatime meal, I would drop to sleep. I couldn't help it. My husband would move me off the sofa at 9 p.m. and put me into bed with my beloved hot water bottle, where I'd recover for the next day of work. Every Tuesday panned out the same — I could not fight the tiredness after each chemotherapy stint. Every Tuesday night, all of us as a family thought that the very next day would be my downfall, but it never came!

On every chemo day, there would be so much sitting around. Sitting around to be called to the chemo bay, then sitting around for six hours and actually having the chemo administered into my body. Before even receiving the chemo, I had to make sure that I had drunk loads of water so that my veins were nice and plump. If they were not, the nurse would find it difficult to source a well-protruding vein. The cannula needle would quickly make a friend with a juicy vein on the top of my hand to administer the drugs as long as I had been a good girl and drunk enough water in the waiting area. The cannula in my hand would get sore. It was also a weird feeling: as the chemo was fed into my vein, it felt like freezing cold liquid travelling up my hand. The veins on my hands are now narrow from the beating that they took from the many needles that chemo brought my way.

You have your chemo medication hanging in a bag on a stand that you have to wheel around whenever you go to the toilet. There is a machine that beeps constantly if there are issues with your medications, or if your medications are running low, or if you unplug your machine for a toilet visit. Sometimes if there's a bubble in the pipe that runs to the cannula in your hand, this makes the machine beep too. A thin pipe carries the chemo medication from the intravenous drip to the cannula in your hand. This machine that monitors the chemo is very annoying! It's super sensitive, and every patient has a machine exactly the same, so there's eight of these highly sensitive beeping devices on each chemo ward. It's all you hear all day long. Beep, beep, beep! It drives the nurses mad, I imagine. It did me. The machine is there for yours and the nurses' benefit, but the pitch and constant sound is irritating. Each chemo bay can accommodate eight patients, and on the ward there are around eight bays. You can literally hear 64 machines demanding the nurses' attention all day long.

The chemo bays have four chairs on each side of the room. Each person has the same set-up, but different types of chemo depending on their cancer. I did not get used to the beeping; as I left hospital I would hear the machines ringing in my ears. Goodness knows how people sleep through it — I couldn't. A chemo day started at 9 a.m. and ended at about 4 p.m. if I was lucky and everything ran according to plan. A long, long, arduous day. I viewed all this travelling to hospital as my new job — the most important job that I would ever do. It was to save my life at the end of the day. What job would I ever do that was more important than this one?

After six weeks of chemo, when I was halfway through my chemotherapy plan, my doctor called me at home on the landline and said that my tumour in my cervix was barely visible. What great words to hear! But I knew another six weeks of chemo, 25 days of radiotherapy and brachytherapy (radiotherapy up inside of my cervix) were still to follow. The phone call was excellent news, but the treatment was only baby steps in.

Hair Loss

When the hospital invited me in to have a discussion about treatment, it involved a conversation about how my body may well suffer; the nurse told me that I would most likely have to accept hair loss. This wasn't a surprise, but it still felt very sad to think that I would have to deal with a bald head for many months. I remember sitting there opposite my oncologist discussing this issue. My husband sat beside me; he mentioned to my oncologist that I had already been thinking about opting for a grey bob-style wig and that we had briefly spoken as a couple about this.

Every week passed, another chemo crossed off, but the hair loss wasn't happening. I would wash it and be really relieved that I couldn't see my beautiful hair in the shower tray, often thinking to myself, "I'm not going to lose my hair — this is fantastic!" The nurses on the chemotherapy ward had also warned me about hair loss on my first appointment.

I was thrilled! Week 5 of chemotherapy came round and I still had hair — not one strand had I seen leave my head. I thought I was going to amaze everybody! Tuesday arrived — this was chemo day every week. I was now on week 5 of chemo and the medication dripped into my veins. "I'm almost there!" I thought.

I sat on my chair and felt quite chipper. I only have today and next Tuesday's chemo to see through, I thought. Next week's chemo marked the end of hair-loss treatment — that was week 6. Week 7 chemotherapy onwards would be a stronger cocktail of poisons but it didn't cause hair loss.

Every week that I turned up to chemo, the nurses would remark, "Aren't you doing well with your hair!" Their faces were always surprised when my hair was still on my head and not showing any signs of falling out. When they said this, I sat there quite confident and smug that my hairstyle, my identity, was going to make it through, that I wasn't going to have to endure a bald head. That Michelle would stay and the bald head that I dreaded wouldn't appear.

No, no, no. By Wednesday of week 5, the very next day after receiving my chemo, my hair started to drop everywhere. All over my home, all over our white Belfast kitchen sink, all over the plates. A few long hairs even managed to drop in our teatime meal that I had cooked! I would gather my hair into a pony-tail style and have about 50 strands of hair in my hand. When hoovering up, I had to pull the hoover pipe towards my body in single strokes to remove my hair from the carpets. This was really annoying more than anything. It was making me so much work. I wasn't upset, I was anxious; I just wanted it gone and fast! It was falling out anyway, and I was so sick of it happening every day.

When I woke up in the mornings, my pillow-case looked like a dog bed. This was pretty sad to look down at; it was absolutely covered in shoulder-length brown hair. As I have mentioned, I was stressed that it was happening all of the time and dropping everywhere, more than being heartbroken that it was falling out — the pace of it leaving my head just wasn't quick enough! This surprised me somewhat, that hair loss was stressing me out, rather than making me cry! I dealt with hair loss brilliantly well.

Quite soon after my hair began to drop out, I thought, "Lose the hair, lose the cancer." I would think of this all the time, my mind helping me to be strong about this serious illness I was carrying around inside my body. The Wednesday, like I have said previously, was when my hair started to leave my head — on the fifth week of receiving chemo. By Saturday, I was so sick of it still happening every day. I put up with this torment from Wednesday right up until Sunday — this is when I'd had enough and took action!

I had a decent hairstyle still, but hair was everywhere in the house! My hairstyle didn't seem to look too bad; it still looked like I had a shoulder-length bob. I could tell though that my hairstyle was really thinning. My problem was not knowing the time frame in which it would totally disappear. This frustrated me; it was like ripping a plaster off very slowly. My husband would constantly say, "You won't lose it all, just stop stressing about it." I wanted it all gone at this point. I was three days away from having my very last hair loss treatment — how annoying, hey! I felt so on edge about my hair being all over the house. I kept saying to my husband, "I'm going to cut it." He'd say, "No, don't!"

It was now Sunday as I've mentioned, and I'd now had to cope with five long days of picking up clumps of hair, hoovering in a ridiculous manner, gathering strands from my clothes on my shoulders, it falling in the shower tray and it being all over my pillow every morning.

This was my chance. My husband fell to sleep on the sofa, and I grabbed the opportunity. I went to the kitchen drawer, found some willing and able scissors, and gave myself a boy's haircut within the space of about 40 minutes. All the time trying to do a decent job whilst Richard was blissfully unaware of my actions. I was hoping he would stay asleep until I had finished. I did this in front of my bedroom mirror, snipping away carefully at my hair of 44 years. I was dreading him waking up, scared of the look on his face and the reaction he was going to give me. He was stunned. I replied, "It's driving me mad, please don't be angry." I WhatsApped my beautiful neighbour Emma and commented, "I have the worst haircut in the village," and she laughed.

I couldn't shape the back of my hair, so a hairdresser neatened it up for me at a local hairdressers. By the time my appointment at the hair salon arrived, around a week on from cutting my hair myself, there was hardly anything left. I warned the hair stylist that there was a shortage of hair under my little navy chemo cap due to my cancer treatment. I'd walked to the shop as it was a sunny day. It wasn't far to walk, and I was booked in for the first early appointment. I hoped to God that I was the only one in the hairdressers.

As I sat down in the chair, I could see her face in the huge salon mirror behind me. With slight trepidation I took off my navy hat and revealed "Baby Chick"! I had named myself this to laugh off losing the hair. I looked like a baby chick due to how sparse my hair had now become. My daughter would say "Baby Chick" when she came for a cuddle, and I would reply, "Cheep cheep!" We would turn the hair loss into a funny memory. My husband and son also got on board and called me Baby Chick too.

I then started wearing big bows or a wig. It was liberating not to have to style or wash my hair. I went heavy on my make-up, and the big bow really suited me. It made me feel so pretty and confident, and I embraced the new look. The new me! When brushing my teeth though, or any moments when I wasn't wearing my wig or bow, that's when I hated the ugliness of having no hair. The sight of my bald head was a constant reminder that I might die, and it felt like a knife was being twisted in my heart.

One thing that really bothered me regarding cancer and treatment was the appearance of my cancer head when people turned up at my door and Richard wasn't there to greet them. My lack of hair took my beauty and femininity, and they were stolen from me at such a testing time in my life. I was dying, and yet cancer was still not happy enough. The cancer medications stripped me of my beauty at my lowest point in life. Not only did cancer want to cheat me, my family and friends of my existence, it also added insult to injury and took my femininity — my hair. I did not let cancer get the one-upmanship regarding this. I embraced no hair and loved the months of the new pretty head bow by finding my own style and rocking my signature look.

When my bow wasn't or couldn't be on my head, that's when it was a stab in the heart. It wasn't pretty, it wasn't positive, it wasn't a picture of health; it was all the opposites of these things. The bald head shouted that cancer was destroying me at that time; I could not run away from this fact.

My bald head was a terrible giveaway, making it obvious to everyone that cancer was inside me. When I didn't want my secret shared, my lack of hair screamed out loud that I had cancer, my baldness blurting out my secret to every stranger! I loved having no hair on the other hand though: no washing it, no styling it, no bad hair days — I just tied a pretty bow or wore my wig and looked fabulous. I loved trying new make-up styles: different shades and colours of make-up seemed to suit me. Bold lipstick, dark eye shadow, red lippy — a newfound favourite. I felt fab in my floral bow — the only issue was that I couldn't get the elastic of the PPE masks offering protection for Covid around my ears. This was a right pain.

I had no hair at all from mid-August 2020 until the end of October 2020. My hair started to reappear in very late October. It looked weird; it looked like when a man really needs a good shave — extremely dark like a five o'clock shadow. Within four weeks, it looked like a crew cut — I was so happy! It was super short but making an appearance. By Christmas it was a short pixie cut. My neighbours remarked through each stage on how much the short hair suited me. Every few weeks, I looked a little different. I thought this part was fun. Now March, it's four inches long all over and has reached the stage where I can't do anything with it. It's long over my ear lobes and a bit wavy. I'm embracing using my hairspray to fluff it out a bit; it looks like a short choppy bob.

I took photos at every stage of my hair growth; I'm really glad I did this. It's a great visual record of how far I have travelled along my journey. The photos of almost no hair and short hair are a fantastic thing to look back on with a sense of relief. It was such a difficult fight but I'm here to tell the tale.

Hold Me Close

This is a very difficult chapter to put pen to paper to — so personal, so dear to my heart. I hope, as I write these feelings down across this page, that I can do justice in my explanations.

The hair started to leave my head, to leave me, to take my beauty — to take Michelle. To take the pretty feminine wife my husband had married 20 years previous. I was always feminine, always dressed wonderfully, and always made an effort to make myself attractive to my adorable husband Richard.

As the hair started to appear sparser, it was my parting that looked as though it was thinning. As I've said, I didn't feel too tearful about losing my hair but it affected me badly when it came to intimate moments. This was, for me, one of the very toughest periods of my journey, to have no hair but still want to give my body to my husband of 20 years. I didn't want to have a non-existent sex life; I didn't want making love to diminish. I wanted to keep the passion the way it had always been: regular, satisfying and full of fun. From the very start of learning about the cancer, I never once wanted to put making love on the shelf.

As my hair began to really thin, when I became Baby Chick, this is when it became a tough battle for me to lay and overcome the cruel appearance that cancer had inflicted on me. To look up at my darling Richard with my almost bald head really split my heart in two. Can you imagine looking into your partner's eyes with no hair? It was so terrible. It tugged so deeply at my heart strings, like 30 rugby players engaging in a game like tug of war.

I wanted to be me. I just wanted to be Michelle. I wanted to look sexy. I wanted Richard to see me, not the cancer, not a dying wife. As I looked at him whilst we made love, I was so desperate to get my health and beauty back. Those moments that we shared between the sheets were so much more loving and tender. Every time I looked into his eyes I was thinking about my horrible cancer appearance, I was thinking about leaving him behind; I couldn't shake it. We were both fully aware that these could be the last acts of love-making as a married couple. Some intimate moments, definitely those early on in my diagnosis, were very emotional rather than enjoyable, as you can well imagine. This part was very difficult for me and Richard to navigate, but we wanted to lavish our love on each other — we didn't know what the following day had in store. It was one of my most heartfelt requests that I wanted us to keep our love life on track as much as possible. Love prevailed; love got us through. I didn't want my husband to look at me and see my bald head. It was so, so tough and upsetting for me to accept this part of cancer.

I did not feel sexy, I did not feel pretty, I did not feel attractive. I wanted to give Richard my body as I always had done, but I knew I was going to have a bald head for a good three months before hair began to show again. I didn't want love-making to come to a halt for three months! It was one of my hardest inner battles to face. I was determined though that cancer was not going to take our sex life away, and I had to find such strength to battle this inner demon. My husband wasn't rocked by my hair loss — he claimed that it wasn't an issue, but it really was for me. I just had to accept that this was the new me for a short while and that the bald head wouldn't be forever. I had to get over this hurdle as quickly as I could so that our sex life could offer us some fun and happiness in this miserable journey we were tangled up in. I hoped and prayed that my hair would grow back swiftly, and it did.

They were such wonderful weeks when my hair finally did start to show. Thank you, my brilliant loving husband, for always making me feel beautiful and loved. Gosh, it's been tough, but because you are my world, you made it easier for me to overcome this challenge. Giving my body and receiving Richard's body seemed so much more intense, more gentle; we were so much more aware of what we might lose! We were both taking part in making love, knowing I might die, fully aware that treatment might not be successful. It was very difficult to engage in a fun enjoyable act as man and wife, but we never gave up; we kept on sharing our souls, our love.

MRI, Radiotherapy, Brachytherapy

The MRI appointments tugged at my heartstrings. These were about 60-minute-long appointments, and along with the journey to get to the appointment and back, each visit took about three hours out of a day. My young body would climb onto the MRI bed and be drawn into the cream tunnel, the machine checking what state my body was in. This was the most accurate way of viewing exactly where the cancer was, how bad it was, and whether my disease was being destroyed.

A mum of 44 years of age, looking so pretty on the outside, it didn't seem real. It didn't seem fair. I would walk through the twists and turns of the corridors and arrive at the MRI suite to accept my time slot, to lie there on this machine worth many thousands of pounds. This was where the positive or negative feedback would be extracted from my body.

Going for MRI check-ups filled me with dread. Were the staff who operated the MRI machine going to see improvements or failings? It seemed unfair that the staff and doctors would see this news before I did. My body, my news — yet I always had to wait for the MRI results. Waiting for news was very demanding of my emotions.

You cannot wear your own clothes when you have an MRI. You have to get changed into sky-blue hospital "scrubs", i.e. the hospital surgery-type PJs like you see actors wear on TV when they work in the operating theatres.

The huge cream tunnel made whistling pulsating noises as my whole body was slowly guided into this extraordinary machine to view the state of my pelvic cancer. The scan would last around 30 minutes. Once inside the tunnel I couldn't see a clock, so I had to count down the minutes using my fingers, sometimes losing count.

The MRI sounds inside the machine were so loud. I wore headphones playing music, but also asked for earplugs. The first time I had an MRI I didn't realise how noisy it was going to be, but the second time and every time after that, I asked for earplugs. I estimate I had around thirteen MRIs in total. The noises the machines made were only comparable to lying down in the middle of roadworks. Beeping, clicking, drilling noises and disturbing loud roadwork noises as the machine moved through its test stages. A lady's voice, computer-like, told me to breathe in and breathe out or to hold my breath for 20 seconds. All very clinical. All very serious. Sometimes my eyes would fill with tears. Tears ran down my temples. Thirty minutes trapped inside this tunnel to think only negative thoughts. When the tears rolled down my temples, I could not wipe them away — my arms were placed close to my body, and the sides of the slim machine stopped me from being able to use my hands to help me dry my tears. I could only let them flow and leave them to dry naturally. The machine made my mind race with thoughts about cancer. I was always anxious about the results and what this machine might flag up. Every MRI was a very worrying experience.

After six weeks of chemotherapy, I started radiotherapy. This would also destroy the cancer inside my body.

Radiotherapy gave me diarrhoea towards the end of the treatment. Having radiation near my bowels was something that I knew may affect me. The radiation was zapping my cervix, my pelvic area, my lymph nodes. It was happening near my bladder too; it was all being risked to reach the cervical cancer.

I had to sign forms to say that I was aware of the possibility of it causing short- and long-term damage to my body. I *had* to sign them; I had no choice: I didn't want cancer in my body. I didn't want cancer to taunt and bully me every day. I wanted it gone forever. I faced a no-win situation. My hand created my signature along the dotted line, the form that stated I agreed and understood that I may be left with life-changing side effects. I didn't want to die, therefore my right hand flowed along, printing my marital name, and accepted the risk. I considered that any side effects would be better than death.

The radiotherapy bed was not very comfortable. It was stiff and hard, comparable to a marble slab. The bed I was lying on was raised up in the air to about five feet, so that the radiotherapy machine could move around the bed and my body, and send radiation waves to the cancer. This did not hurt. The radiotherapy only took about two minutes but the total prep and travel to the hospital and back sapped up half a day, every day, for five weeks.

Every day was like groundhog day during those 25 days of

radiotherapy. It was tough for me to accept that I had to put my body through this torture — inflicting damage on my organs because of cancer. My faithful body had given me memories, life, children, and all the other wonderful things I'd achieved. Now here I was, having to punish it with radiation. It felt cruel.

There I sat in the radiotherapy waiting area: happy, smiling, big bow on my head, make-up on, looking glam. It didn't seem real that I had to be there. I wasn't in a state; I didn't look ill. I would swan in and out as upbeat as I could possibly be; I wanted to stay happy and bubbly for all who cared for me. Thank you, body. How did you rise above such black treatment? I am so proud of how you coped, although I really was the best mum that I could be to you. I gave you everything you needed: well-earned sleep, positivity and a fabulous diet.

On arriving at radiotherapy, I had to make sure I was well hydrated — I had to drink a sports bottle full of water within five minutes and then sit for 50 minutes and wait for the fluid to reach my bladder. The fullness of my bladder made my cervix a certain shape and position. I always had to have the same measure of urine in my bladder for all 25 sessions of my radiotherapy treatment. This was so that the radiotherapy hit the correct area inside my body. My treatment plan stated that it was vital for my bladder to have the exact amount of fluid showing on the monitor every time I received radiation. My bowels had to be empty too; I couldn't eat food that created gas. Again, this was because full bowels or gas would make my insides a different shape, and the treatment had been designed for my body to look exactly the same inside on every single session. Even losing weight slightly altered the way that the computers read my treatment markers. Body gas and the wrong measurement in my bladder would have affected the shape of my cervix and delayed treatment.

The first few times that I received treatment, I had too much urine in my bladder. The staff asked if I could stop a wee mid-flow! I replied, "No," and laughed. On returning home, I decided that this might be a useful skill for further treatments — after all, I had another 24 to experience yet! I decided my homework would be to master the skill of stopping my wee mid-flow! I managed this technique within a day — I was very proud of myself. The radiotherapy staff were very impressed at my homework. We all had many a laugh about it. Every time I went for my radiotherapy, I would ask the radiotherapy staff, "How much wee would you like me to get rid of?" The radiotherapy girls would tell me how far up a white plastic disposable cup to wee to get rid of the perfect amount of urine so that treatment could go ahead swiftly. My homework really helped with how speedily the treatment was carried out.

The staff would use ultrasound to see how full my bladder was. I had to lie very still and not move on the radiotherapy bed. The staff lined up my body with lasers on the machine above me. On knowing you are going to have radiotherapy, you have to have tiny tattoo markers on your body — between the breasts, on the hips and above the pubic bone area — so that the treatment goes to the exact same place every time you receive radiation. The lasers and tattoo markers reassure the radiographers that the radiotherapy is targeting the exact place where the cancer is growing. None of the treatment for radiotherapy causes pain.

On the radiotherapy bed, my arms had to be placed above my head in a ballerina position. The team at radiotherapy make each patient a special pillow (a moulded pillow that dries hard, especially for your personal arm pose). Each patient has their own pillow each time they receive treatment.

The effect of radiotherapy for me was that drinking so much water in five minutes made me very bloated and windy after treatment. I had to drink ginger in hot water, take peppermint capsules daily, and constantly suck antacid tablets. Being full of wind in the abdominal area plagued my every day for 25 days. Every day from around 2 p.m. until the middle of the night, I would feel as full as a balloon, with pains. The radiation was hitting the bottom part of my stomach too, so this was also to blame for me feeling so rough and windy.

Brachytherapy was my last type of treatment. I absolutely dreaded it. Radiotherapy in my lady bits! I didn't know what to expect but I wasn't looking forward to it.

I arrived at the Royal Derby Hospital at 7.15 a.m. on Tuesday 24th September 2020. I met the Brachytherapy team who would be looking after me. I didn't know any of them. This made me feel very lonely, although the team tried their hardest to lift my mood. We walked along and finally reached an empty ward. The Covid pandemic had made everything very clinical and empty. Nobody was around apart from me and three members of staff who asked me to get undressed and into a hospital gown, and then climb onto on a hospital bed ready to go to theatre. I was very scared; many frightening thoughts and feelings were present that day. My oncologist appeared and stood by my bed and asked me to sign forms. I was so grateful to see her familiar face. An anaesthetist came and explained that it was best to opt for an epidural in my spine for pain relief. I went with the flow.

By this point it was only about 7.40 a.m. I was sitting up on a hospital bed waiting for the theatre staff to arrive for their daily shift in the operating theatre. Finally, after lots of preparation, the staff wheeled me into theatre. Oh my days, I was so scared! My mind and heart were racing; I didn't know what to expect. I was told to sit forwards for the epidural. This was to numb the lower half of my body. My hospital bed was pushed through a set of double doors where I saw lots of surgeons waiting, along with huge bright lights on the theatre ceiling. The epidural had taken effect and I didn't feel completely with it. The surgeons worked their magic and fitted radiotherapy rods around my cervix, where the radiation would destroy the last remains of cancer.

I was then wheeled to the MRI suite to have imagery taken to make sure that the rods had been positioned correctly. I then went to radiotherapy where I received radiation into my cervix. This didn't hurt; it was just a feeling of buzzing. It lasted 5 to 10 minutes; I don't recall the time span. At 9 a.m. I was taken onto a ward three floors higher than the radiotherapy zone, where the pain started to kick in. It was a pain of pressure, like a baby crowning — the exact same pain. Thank goodness the hospital allocated me a private room.

The brachytherapy procedure involves the rods being packed with gauze so that they stay against the sides of the cervix. The radiotherapy then travels through these rods and is administered to the area where cancer is a concern. I assumed the baby crowning pain that I was experiencing was to do with pressure — the pressure of the radiotherapy rods being held in place so that they wouldn't move over the course of this treatment.

As lunchtime approached, I'd had my fill of morphine. As I have previously mentioned, thank goodness that I was lucky enough to have privacy in my own room. I asked for help with the pain and a nurse offered me paracetamol. She informed me that I had been administered my quota of morphine and that this was now my only option of pain relief. I went quiet for a second, as the thought of no more morphine was difficult to cope with. I accepted the paracetamol and replied that it would at least assist with my back pain, which was present due to lying flat and still for a good few hours.

Because of the rods, I had to stay in bed. I had to have a catheter bag fitted as I couldn't get up for the toilet. This process was painless. It was done in theatre, when the pain relief was at its best. The radiotherapy rods that were up inside my cervix meant that I couldn't move, sit or bend or even get off of my bed! The hospital bed that I spent 34 hours on was electronic and tilted, so if I wanted to alter the position of my bed it only pivoted. I was always lying flat; I didn't bend once in 34 hours. The whole trunk of my body remained flat throughout my hospital stay.

I soon realised that this treatment was going to be difficult to bear! Even turning over was a no-no on my own. By teatime, I was shattered. I'd been wheeled down again to radiotherapy for a second round of radiation to my cervix. I couldn't move; this was the toughest thing I had ever endured! It was a nightmare. My back and leg pain was intense because I couldn't get up and walk around. It was now midnight and I'd been on the same bed since 7.30 that morning without moving or bending. I drifted in and out of consciousness. I nodded on and off for about two hours in total. I had to get a nurse to put my socks on; I was helpless and restless.

My older sister was texting me all of the time at this point — thank goodness she was my support. She offered me distraction, which I so badly needed through the hours of unrest. Throughout my cancer journey my sister has been very supportive and for this I am truly grateful. Thank you, Melanie, for phoning and texting every day. I really appreciated your time and dedication to my well-being at such a worrying period in my life.

Through the night I asked for heat packs for my spine and tummy. My legs and back were killing me. I had to cling onto the side rails of the hospital bed just to slightly move. I was so scared of doing this, as I knew that rigid rods were placed up inside my pelvic area. I didn't want to cause any lasting damage, and the medical staff had made it very clear that I should not move without four nurses assisting me. I did grab my rails without the nurses though, as I was in so much pain. My back and the bedsheets were so clammy from lying there so long. This was the toughest thing I had ever tolerated.

The next day was a repeat performance — the same treatment all over again. In fact, the second day was even worse because my body was suffering even more pain than the day before due to not being able to move about. The treatments happened at 9 a.m. and 4 p.m. The pain was escalating all the time. In total, I was laid flat on a bed for 34 hours without moving, bending or sitting! I couldn't climb out of bed or sit up or walk about due to the rigid rods that had been fitted in theatre. The experience was incredibly challenging, I tell you.

By 5.30 p.m. I was in my own room with the rods removed — thank goodness! I was frightened to climb off of the bed and move my stiff legs around the room, but when I did it felt heavenly. To be able to simply walk with freedom felt fabulous. As I walked around my room it felt tremendous to take those baby steps and use my poor legs. God, I was proud of myself — this was a hospital visit never to be forgotten.

At 6 p.m. I told a nurse that I wanted to go home. She said, "Oh, I'm not sure we can discharge you." I was ready for home. I had my belongings packed, my head bow on board and make-up applied. I wanted out of there ASAP! I told the nurse I'd phoned my husband already and that he was on his way to collect me. A little white lie, but I deserved it after the 34 hours I had just endured! The ward agreed to send me home.

My wonderful oncologist came to say well done before I was discharged, and I think she was also hoping in her heart that she wouldn't see me again, as this would mean that treatment had been a success.

Richard came to the ward to collect me, and we walked out at 7 p.m. — what an encounter! The funny thing was that Richard had forgotten his mask that had to be worn because of the Covid pandemic. He had a genius idea and wore his hoodie back to front, using his hood as a mask. When I spotted this, I was in fits of laughter.

So just to elaborate, I arrived at 7.15 a.m. on a Tuesday, got on the hospital bed at 7.30 a.m. and didn't climb off the hospital bed until 5.30 p.m. Wednesday teatime. It was one of the most difficult challenges that I have EVER been presented with.

I have to add this very funny story. When Richard and I went dog walking one day, he made up a rhyme about my up-and-coming brachytherapy. He said I was having brachy up my cracky! Oh my Lord, we were killing ourselves with laughter in the open fields as our dog flitted about getting her daily fix on nature's treasure hunt.

When I was lying in my bed on the Wednesday of my procedure, this is when I'd been in bed for more than 28 hours, three brachytherapy nurses were assigned to look after me, helping me with the pain that my body felt all over. I had to find something to lift my mood and spur me on, so I told the three nurses of this rhyme that my husband had made up. We were all killing ourselves with laughter, although there was one male nurse who must have felt very outnumbered! The laughing hurt my lady bits so much, but it was worth it to share my husband's wit! They must have thought, "Flipping heck, we've got a right fruit loop here!" At this point in time when the rhyme was shared they understood my character quite well though; this was now the second day that they'd been looking after me as best as they could. The three brachytherapy staff members who were by my bedside most of the time were absolute treasures. These ladies were another three angels that I met along my cancer hike.

This was the ONLY and I mean ONLY smile I displayed in all 34 hours of my visit for my brachytherapy procedure.

Lifesaver

C ancer came, and we threw caution to the wind. I asked my husband to buy a motorbike so that we could go out and make memories together. He fulfilled my request. I was in my third week of chemo at this point. We didn't know when or if chemo was going to floor me or lay me in the ground.

It was only a cheap motorbike — good condition though. It had low mileage and was powerful enough to make me smile and make my heart bubble over with joy. A red Yamaha MT-03 — it was a really classic-looking bike and was a real head-turner. It didn't show its age. I loved it. It had style and grunt. It was going to offer us a lot of happiness, but we didn't know this at the time — we were just hoping it was. We had racked up a gap of 17 years without a motorbike, so we were very dubious.

My husband took a trip out to Bottesford to look at the bike in question. I was excited. I was having chemotherapy all of that day, so Richard went to view it along with his dad. They looked at it and left a deposit. When I came home from treatment Richard informed me that my dream request was beginning to unfurl! He had found the two wheels that would play a massive part in my recovery! I was more than excited to clap eyes on the hero that I was pinning all my hopes on to lift my depression.

A few days later, myself, Richard, Trinity and my sporty beast drove to collect this bike. It looked stunning and it sounded beautiful when Richard started it up. It made my heart beat with curiosity — was I going to love being pillion in the way that I had done 17 years previous? Yes, I was! Oh, MT-03, how I loved you!

The people that we bought the MT-03 off were so nice. The lady, Charlotte, who owned the bike, was full of nostalgia. She had owned this beauty for 13 years. It must have been tough for her to see Richard climb on and drive it away. But she could see that we loved it — that we needed it. She knew that I was poorly, as Richard had mentioned this to her when he handed over the deposit.

Richard rode the motorbike back home while I followed behind in my car. My daughter was sitting beside me. We both watched with pride and joy as Richard rode his new bike home. I wasn't thinking about cancer at all at that point, I was just so eager to jump on the back of the bike. To see whether or not it could shower me with bags of happiness. All the way home I was thinking, "I hope it's not going to be a waste of money."

About five days later, once Richard felt confident and safe enough to add me as a passenger, it was time! It was time for me to sit at the back of Richard. I was filled with many feelings: fear, excitement, and the longing for the thrill that a motorbike offers you! We were rusty the first few times out. The first time ever climbing onto the MT-03, my heart was doing somersaults, reverting back to when we owned a stunning sparkly bright blue Fazer motorbike — this was around 2004. Many years had slipped by since this had been our thrill-seeking hobby.

Back then, Richard and I loved it so much, but we had two tiny, yummy children to look after, and the rides and speeds weren't fair on them. The risk of something happening to us both was a risk we weren't willing to take. So, we had to give up our kicks, our love. It was for good reason — the time had come to be selfless, not selfish.

But here we were, many years on, a wise, established married couple with cancer snapping at my life span. I was now witnessing a desperate, committed husband willing to pull out every stop to make me feel alive and see me smile. Our first trip out was to a place called Codnor to a Tesco superstore. Here, we purchased a meal deal. This was the very first time that Richard asked me, "What do you think?" We had parked up and I had climbed off the back of the MT-03. My reply, with a huge smile on my face: "I love it!" Oh, that makes my eyes well up as I type that. I didn't know then how special and important riding out was going to be. We rode a lot further and had a picnic by the gate of a roadside farm in the sun, on the outskirts of Matlock. We sat on our motorbike jackets eating our lunch on the ground, our first ever outing — it was amazing! We talked about how great it felt to be back on a bike again after so many years had passed by. We both said what a great chapter this was going to offer us, and that we were going to get out on the MT-03 as much as we could.

I couldn't get enough of it. The racer chick blood ran deep inside my body still. It was thrilling; it made me forget about my cares. These were the moments when I could be me, not Michelle worrying about cancer. I would sit on the back of the bike travelling at 70 mph thinking this is madness, but superb. The speeds, the bends, the overtaking — it made me feel alive! It topped up my empty heart with the happiness that it lacked and desired. The bike recharged my heavy heart to a happy fluttering one again every time we used it. The motorbike trips would offer me the hugest boost of adrenaline; it was like a drug and a fabulous friend to me, all in one ride out. I used to think — and still do when we go out — I bloody love it, this is fabulous, whoo-hoo! When we were out on the motorbike though, it would dawn on me; I would think, "Are we out on the bike all the time because I might die? Is my husband pulling out all the stops because I might die?" The answer was a very clear YES to both questions. We didn't know if treatment would work. We didn't know if I would see Christmas. We didn't know if we would celebrate our 21st wedding anniversary.

I'd close my eyes round daring islands and bends and forget my cancer and suck up the fun, excitement and exhilaration of the ride. I'd truly enjoy my arms being around my husband's waist — we looked the business. We looked a great team; we were out doing this. "Screw you, cancer," I would think. I would look at the back of my husband's neck and think how truly lucky I was and am! My darling, doing this for me, trying to please me in every way possible. I'd glance again at his neck and be totally overwhelmed that he was mine. He'd tap my knee to warn me that we were going to pick up speed and I'd think YESSS — go on, I'm ready, go for it, let's pick off these cars in front of us. What fun! Here it came, the speed, the power, the absolute buzz only a motorbike at speed can offer.

Most days we would get dressed into our leather riding gear and Richard would wheel out the MT-03, ready for our fix. Again, it was teamwork — my hubby and I enjoying each other. There are few sights that make me grin every time I see them, but when the wheels of the motorbike are moving without the engine running, I know that happiness and thrills are imminent.

About four weeks in from having this bike, we rode to a dealership to have a look for a new helmet for me. I had no hair by now — under my helmet sat my bare scalp, and when I removed my helmet I was totally bald. I used to tie a chiffon headscarf around my neck, then on arrival take off my helmet and tie a bow on my head in my husband's motorbike wing mirror. One particular day that I did my usual trick, the car park was packed with men, ogling at each other's motorbikes. I removed my helmet and quickly created my bow in the tiny mirror. Fiddling away to make it look decent, I completed my artwork — my bow. Richard looked at me and said, "I just love how you are brave enough to do that." I replied, "I have no choice. I can't walk around the shop with my helmet on — I'll look a right moron, won't I?" I smiled at him and laughed. We walked into the shop together holding hands — we weren't letting cancer hide me away.

I spotted a helmet that I really wanted. I knew it was going to be awkward asking to try it on; I knew I would have to take off my bow and show this middle-aged man behind the sales desk my cancer head. I did it though. The man didn't know where to look. I placed the helmet that I had taken a liking to onto my bald head: it fitted perfectly. I took it to the checkout desk to pay for it.

Richard followed me then pulled out his debit card and treated me to it. Richard was so impressed at how brave I had been that day that he treated me to my new lid. Thank you, cancer — you saved me £179 that day.

Fast forward another six weeks and I had four weeks of radiotherapy under my belt. The treatment can often affect patients' bowels, and sometimes gives you a dicky tummy. This was affecting me — I wasn't going to let this stop my motorbike antics with Richard, though. I had to think outside the box and think smart. I was immunocompromised at the time and couldn't mix or shop in busy places, so this brainwave was brilliant! I sent my poor husband to look for this product that I needed, this new shopping list item. What was it? I am hearing you ask. The product was female incontinence pants!

If I was on the back of Richard's motorbike and needed to go, I might not have had time for him to pull over. Radiotherapy had given me an upset tummy towards the end and sometimes when I was passing wind I was worrying somewhat! Running to the toilet was not an option when flying along tarmac roads at high speeds. Nothing, and I mean nothing, was going to stop me having motorbike fun with my hero!

So, my only option was to wear these female incontinence pants, which meant I was able to carry on getting my kicks of happiness that I knew were the reason for me coping so outstandingly with such black thoughts, topping up my trampled heart with the adrenaline the motorbike offered in abundance. Under my gorgeous red leather trousers were crucial toddler-like pull-up pants, but it was my little secret. I was able to fly along sitting on the pillion seat regardless of radiotherapy's drawbacks.

I would use my trusty red rucksack for my spare incontinence pants and a loo roll, but I never experienced an underwear accident, thank goodness. My tummy never decided to be that evil at high speeds, and I never pooped my pants. YAY! I wasn't going to let cancer or radiotherapy spoil my motorbike joy.

I decided to use my wig for bike trips out. Even going on picnics to the roadside for a trip out, getting fuel, or nipping in for a wee somewhere involved removing my helmet, thereby revealing my cancer to the world. This is something that I found really difficult. I was not brave enough back then in 2020 to show my bald head to strangers. I felt it was my secret and I didn't want to shout about it. If we were out on motorbike trips, once my helmet was removed I would quickly fit my wig on my head. I didn't want many people knowing I was so ill, and I kept it very private from July 2020 to March 2021. My friend, the trusty red rucksack, was my passenger on motorbike journeys, and there inside the rucksack waited my faithful confidant, "Wiggy". It covered my biggest, deepest, most personal secret — my illness.

As soon as we hit our destination, out would pop my cover-up to assist me in getting rid of my ugly appearance and shielding me from total strangers drawing the quick conclusion that I was a cancer victim out on a motorbike. That must have looked so crazy to onlookers. It must have seemed that I was made of iron. I put the wig on swiftly as we pulled up to places. My cancer was inside, but once my hair fell out there was no hiding it. Once my bald head was on display, all who saw me knew I had cancer. The bald head revealed my biggest, deepest, most intimate secret that I was trying to keep to myself as much as possible. You have no way at all of hiding your illness — even a headscarf, my bow, screamed cancer to strangers. It was really only the wig that truly hid my demon.

The first time I tried Wiggy under my helmet was in our village before we had a ride out. I had visions that I could wear Wiggy under my helmet, then on arriving at our destination I could pull off my helmet and reveal a perfect hairstyle. This plan did not go well — not at all. I pulled off my brilliantly fitting helmet (as it well should be — it's there to save your brain were you ever to be involved in a motor accident); off came my helmet and so did Wiggy! My husband and I laughed so much; the plan was a big fat fail. There Wiggy sat, nestled comfortably in the top of my helmet, and there I stood with the scalp that I had planned to disguise!

Thank you, Wiggy, for keeping my secret from the world when we were out on day trips. You travelled in my rucksack at great speeds, ready to help me enjoy my afternoons out. I don't imagine many cancer wigs have been on a motorbike at 70 mph! My little Wiggy must reside in the minority surely, the speeds at which it flew along on my back.

Spine Chills

When I went for a shower in the evenings, this is where I sometimes cried long and hard. The shower was the place I released my fears and anxiety of death, hoping that the fan for ventilation and my very loud music that I played in the shower would drown out the sound of my breakdowns. It became an art to shield my family from sadness once I'd mastered this plan. I would take my Flip speaker, hoping that it was loud enough to mask out my desperate unhappiness, my fears of dying.

I'd scuttle off like a rat, offloading my deepest pain; leaving them all was an unbearable scenario. I would play my favourite song so bloody loud to disguise my endless sobbing. There I would stand under the hot waterfall, shedding my worry and shielding my family. The soap in my palm, circling it into my skin and thinking to myself, "What is the path ahead for me?" When I moved the soap around my slim suffering body, I hated the point at which I washed the cancer area, my tummy. The very thought that my hands were passing over the area where cancer thrived was like wringing out a flannel, only the flannel was my heart, and I was in such agony. I didn't want to be cancer's host and I certainly didn't want to be its victim!

The one thing that saved me in all these desperate periods whilst having showers was my favourite song, Rui Da Silva – Touch Me. Oh, I played this song so bloody loud! The feel-good factor it offered up never once failed me. I would sing the words enthusiastically to lift my spirits, to stop the tears flowing. This song was my only best friend when I could not show my tears to my family. The song was my handkerchief. The words, I bloody love them — listen to them and soak them up! Each line is so true, and each line I dedicate to my wonderful best friend: my husband. I didn't want my time with him to be up. I didn't want to leave him. I wanted many more years with my darling Richard. I wanted to see my children grow and prosper. I wanted to see my future grandchildren look into my eyes as I pushed them along in a brand new pram. I couldn't bear the thought of slipping away from them all.

You think it's a dance song, but it's a song about love and closeness, a song of intimacy between two people, two best friends, two lovers. Each line is so true and special, each line makes me think of Richard, each line is amazing. It is my favourite song EVER! Even above my wedding songs, it means that much to me. It's my cancer survival song. It's my journey song. It's my addiction song. It's my friend when I needed a hug song. It's the song that put its arms around me and squeezed me tight when nobody else could. It's a song that will run through my veins forever.

This song made me feel high when I was at my lowest; it's my turn-my-emotions-around song. This song was my parent when my family didn't know I was breaking down. The song put my heart back together again. The words remind me of my deep endless love for my Richard. He's my rock, my world. Each line of the song is for him. Each line is me singing it to my best friend.

I will never tire of hearing this song. It's another amazing friend who supported me through the lowest time in my life. I even messaged Rui Da Silva on Facebook to tell him this.

Magical Village

Covid-19 made work steadier for us, and I didn't mind. Because of this, I decided to make more effort in the village and unite neighbours more. I had cancer now; I didn't mind if people thought, "Why is Michelle arranging events?" Cancer was my worry now, I just wanted some village fun. It was bonfire night, and Covid-19 had stopped all displays from happening. Myself, Emma and Emily arranged sparklers on the village road, I made bonfire toffee, and another neighbour supplied mulled wine. Most of the village was involved — it was great. We all whirled our sparklers round like ten-year-old children. It was cold, but fun. As I handed out the toffee, I felt a little bashful, but what a great start to bringing the village closer together.

I didn't know, but there would be one thing that would become a total love; an escape; a building block for health and friendship and well-being. This was walking. First, my husband and I would constantly walk every day as lockdown didn't allow much activity. Then, it would also offer me a massive friendship with a neighbour I only used to wave to. I have already told you about this beautiful part of my journey, where I bonded with my dear friend Emma.

In those very first terrible weeks, my husband and I walked for miles. We were overwhelmed and shocked. We'd talk, we'd hold hands, we would enjoy the walks and enjoy each other. The future was uncertain, that was for sure. Fortunately, we lived in a very peaceful village with green fields all around us and walks on our doorstep. I went from walking a few miles a day to walking around 8 miles a day; I'd walk with my husband and our dog and then another walk would follow with my neighbour Emma. It would be nothing strange for me to walk 8 miles a day in the months of November 2020 to February 2021.

Next on the list of events was a Christmas tree competition. We girls wanted to purchase a huge tree for the village green, but it worked out too costly. Emily, Emma and I told the village neighbours if they wanted to play along, to buy a small tree of their own and place it on the village green all trimmed up. The postman would judge the winning tree, and the winner would receive a prize. At the same time, we asked the whole village to decorate the outside of their houses with Christmas lights. Most took part, and the village looked fabulous. One of my neighbours had her retired husband up their 20-foot conifer tree that stood in their front garden. We set a date for our first ever village Christmas lights switch-on — wow, it was brilliant! So many neighbours came out in the dark to be part of the switch-on; lights danced everywhere. I hope we can build on this display every year!

Also around December, I purchased binoculars. I decided to make homemade bird feeders. This was a winter project; something to distract me from cancer. I chose an area of trees and claimed it as my bird-feeding station. I was looking after nature; maybe God would notice. It felt wonderful giving to the birds; I loved filling the feeders and watching them feed. I would sit out there in the middle of the village green, all wrapped up — it was freezing! Some days I bird watched when snow was on the ground. A cup of tea in my hand, huge coat, snow boots, gloves, hat and scarf. I loved to see the birds playing and gathering the seed that I had provided for them. Neighbours would come over to me and chat and say, "Aren't you cold?" I would reply, "Yes, but I'm happy here watching the birds play and feed." I embraced nurturing nature. I would see robins and hope it was a sign of my mam sending her love from heaven.

One night in December 2020, it was after teatime I would estimate, the sky began to bless our pretty village with fresh falling snow. It was cold and peaceful, and nobody in the village was leaving this place. They were all hunkered down in their cosy houses and tucked up for the evening. I opened my front porch door to witness beautiful white rough-edged dollops of snow falling on my drive and doormat.

I knew full well what was going to happen next. My neighbours were most definitely going to start messaging me to ask if I had spotted the latest weather. My phone started to ping, and it was Emma and Emily asking, "Have you looked out of your window? It's snowing!" Grown women, giddy at the sight of this winter weather; they were like excited puppies!

The messages asked if we were meeting up on the village green for a cuppa to enjoy the new spectacle. Their messages were filled with joy, and we all agreed to get wrapped up and meet at the bench near the lamp post that threw out a calming orange hue onto the unadopted road on which we live.

I walked towards the bench. I had a fawn faux fur blanket tucked under my arm, and I walked slowly so that I would not spill my hot chocolate all over my glove on my hand. I was thinking it was going to be freezing out there, so I was prepared with this lush warm blanket from my living room chair. I was, and am not, that keen on snow — it makes our village very difficult to leave.

It was so special though. Emma and Emily both adore the snow and they were giddy with glee; their faces said it all. Two addictive smiles looking at me that made the memory so much more magical. Their faces were beacons of happiness, these two mature women acting the age of infants.

The streetlamp near the bench where we had decided to sit made the snow appear a peach haze. Everywhere was so steady and still. Emma stood up and jumped about on the spot to keep warm while Emily and I sat on the bench. Our legs were so toasty covered by the blanket I had provided.

The faux fur charcoal grey coat I had opted to wear was keeping me so comfy I wasn't cold at all. I had a huge fluffy faux fur grey hat to match. I could have stayed there all evening, chatting and enjoying their friendship. My coat began to change colour as the snow settled on my shoulders and arms; it now appeared a pale grey. The flakes of snow fell so fast, and they were as large as chocolate buttons; it was majestic.

That memory, to this day, is perfection. Emma laughed out loud as she stood and looked at us both on the wooden bench. The blanket on our legs had a thick layer of snow on it by now, and she commented that we looked like we belonged in a scene from Narnia. How idyllic.

This is a trinket box memory. We sat out there for ages. Our breath could be seen in the cold crisp air, and snow was now all over the road. All three of us remarked that this was a special place to grow old in; we were so lucky to be gathered there in our little friendship circle.

I'm not a lover of snow but I am of this memory. I really hope that snow comes again this year so that we can mimic last year's beautiful, glorious image that sits way deep in my mind.

My Mirror Image, My Soul Sister Martina

There I sat in my chair at chemotherapy. It was a Tuesday. It was my third week there and around the end of July 2020. I sat in one of the hospital chairs that I have mentioned in another chapter. The chemotherapy drip was pushed into the top of my hand, administering the drugs into my bloodstream. There I sat, willingly, accepting this awful concoction that killed good and bad cells. What a crazy, terrible thought! But there was no option but to go down this route.

Surrounded by other patients, all having chemotherapy, there I sat, young and vibrant, longing to go home. I was 44 years of age — what the hell! I felt like I had been placed there to watch over the ward.

I spotted a female across from where I was sitting. She was also receiving chemotherapy. She was on a hospital bed though, her curtains drawn around her bay for privacy with just enough of a gap for me to realise that she was around my age. A tiny part of my heart was overjoyed; I know that sounds terrible because she was also sick, but in my heart and mind I thought she could well be somebody that I could strike up a conversation with if I saw her in the weeks to follow at our chemotherapy sessions. I longed for a friend on treatment days, you see. There were only ever older people next to me, and this made me feel very singled out.

It was refreshing to see a younger person in my bay. I did not know at this point just how very important this stranger who was lying across from me would become. There it was; that was our minuscule glance in this large world in which we lived. I was clocking my soon-to-be sister, my mirror image. I kept hearing the nurses calling her name as they asked her questions — "Martina", I heard the nurses saying. What a beautiful name, I thought. I assumed she was shy. I assumed she didn't want to befriend any other patients on the chemo ward, as why else would she have her curtains drawn around the bed?

A few weeks passed and I was waiting for my first radiotherapy session. I sat there in the reception. As I sat there, I heard a lady's voice, bubbly and upbeat. I looked up; the very same lady was checking into reception and asking if they could keep an eye on her little boy. She had brought him with her as she had no childcare; she had no option but to attend her radiotherapy treatment with her young son in tow. I felt sorry for her that this was her only option. I smiled and nodded at her and said "hello".

She had such a kind smile and a Slovakian accent. She said "hello" back.

She was dressed in a trendy manner — a baggy modern sweat jumper, black skinny jeans, a big trendy leather bag and white flat pumps. I thought, "Oh, she's a trendy mum." Off she went for her treatment; I would see her again a week later but this I wasn't aware of.

The next week, I started up a conversation with her, only to find out that she had exactly the same cancer as me! I was so thrilled to be able to talk to her about our diagnosis, as at least we had this one thing in common.

Over the next weeks, I would see her many times in the radiotherapy waiting area; I would look forward to going to my treatment appointments in case she was also there. Often, she was there. It was wonderful to sit and build our relationship, and I really warmed to her. She was 42 years of age. Soon we were such good pals. We would always ask each other what times our radiotherapy was scheduled for. We started to become really close. I loved her aura.

She only lost a little of her hair on top whereas I had lost all of mine by now. We would laugh about my wigs and bows, and she would tell me which she liked the best. She really loved this one particular wig I wore. She loved the blonde highlights that ran through the short brown wig. She was the sunshine of my hospital visits; she made the painful waiting around such fun, and the feeling was mutual. Every time I sat with her I would love her a little bit more.

On my twenty-fifth session of radiotherapy treatment, she was there again. She was so pleased for me that it was my very last appointment. I offered her my mobile number; she took the scrap of paper and put it into her bag. On that day she gave me such a massive cuddle, she was so delighted that hospital appointments were over for me for a good few months. I stood closely opposite her after we had stopped hugging and said that we were going to get told off for hugging because we were breaking Covid rules, although we weren't mixing with anybody else due to being immunocompromised by chemotherapy.

I was overjoyed when she contacted me. This was a week later when I was on my way to hospital to receive my very final treatment, brachytherapy, which I was very dubious about having. I was so touched when I received a good luck text from her. I was scared of what I was about to go through and this message from her was a dose of love to spur me on.

We used Messenger to communicate, as now I wasn't attending hospital. I received a message from her once a week. She would message me every Saturday evening; it felt like Christmas when Saturday nights arrived. This was the one night in the week that she would get in touch with me. I knew this was when she would let me know a little snippet of her life and how her health was unfolding. The once-a-week messages kept happening up until New Year's Eve of 2020.

On New Year's Eve 2020, she worried me somewhat when she revealed to me in a message that she had found a lump in her armpit. This would be the downward spiral for my poor, dear friend Martina. In the first week of 2021, we picked up our game and messaged daily. She had realised by now that I was a friend she could trust; a friend she could confide in; a friend she could rely on. I would tell her how I was filling my days — how Richard and I were whizzing around on the motorbike. She would call me a "stupid bitch" for a laugh. The friendship was like sisterhood. She also liked to call me a "crazy bitch".

She would tell me about her days and how her new job was unfolding, how her little boy was doing at school, and what the hospital had got planned for her cancer treatments moving forwards. She was now having to come to terms with the news that she had secondary cancer. She would often say the pain was making her daily life difficult. Above all though, we clicked so wonderfully together. The phone calls and voice messages were becoming like those that sisters share.

At this point, I didn't know if my treatment had worked. We went on messaging each other constantly — five or six times a day, every day. Now it was 19th February 2021, my MRI scan day. This was to see if the treatment had worked inside my body. I had the MRI and arranged to meet Martina at hospital as she lived in Derby and was only a five-minute drive away from where I was going to be attending.

We met in the car park. Bear in mind that I hadn't seen her personally since the end of September 2020, which was when I'd handed her my mobile contact details. It was now 19th February 2021. I was bursting to see her, longing to have a cuddle, and so excited to be in her presence. Martina was anxious about meeting up. I asked, "Why are you feeling this way?" She replied, "I don't know." She was just so private, you see, and didn't let anybody into her life. We had by now racked up a gap of five months of not physically sitting next to each other. There was no need for her to worry. She walked across the car park; my eyes picked her out in the distance and I waved frantically to her. She walked quickly towards me and threw her arms around me. It was wonderful to hug my "virtual sister". It was so amazing to be in her presence, to squeeze her Puffa coat and to embrace her. To have her beating heart close to mine. Oh my goodness, we were such a happy pair of bunnies dashing across the car park, smiling at each other and chatting away as we walked to where we had parked. We were grown women acting like little schoolgirls who were best friends in a playground.

The car park had maybe 600 cars parked in it, maybe even more. Guess where Martina had parked? At this point she was totally clueless about the car that I drove around in. Yes, she had parked right next to mine; out of all those spaces at the Royal Derby Hospital that she could have chosen, there sat her little grey Peugeot next to my beast! Our bloody cars alongside each other, it was a sign — a very special one from above, I believe!

There we sat in the car park, on an area of lawn near some trees. We had taken chairs, drinks and snacks for the afternoon, but before we knew it, it was time to pack away and part company. Two hours had flown by, and it had felt like ten minutes!

About three weeks later, she came to visit me at home in my village. She brought me a huge bunch of vibrant coloured flowers and a garden snail ornament as my birthday was looming. She loved the snail she had brought me so much that she purchased herself one for her own garden. She jokingly called it "Turbo", and I in turn called mine "Power" so that the names linked together. My birthday visit from Martina was so special.

By now, we started and ended our messages to each other by typing "Hi sis" and "Bye sis"; we were very close and loved each other dearly. Each week that passed, she would get different concerning symptoms, to my sadness. It wasn't looking rosy for my beautiful Martina, and this pained my heart. I could do nothing more than be a great friend to her; I know this meant the world to her. She admitted to me on many occasions that she didn't open up to people and that her main focus was her husband and little boy. She was from Slovakia and her husband from the Czech Republic. They kept themselves to themselves. They looked out for each other.

When I heard I was free of cancer on 16th March, hers was the fourth phone number that I dialled. I called my son, daughter, my in-laws of 21 years, and then I called my soul sister Martina. I cried as I told her my fabulous news, as by this point they had told Martina that she was getting worse and would need more chemo and that it was in her bones and lymph nodes.

She knew that I was attending the hospital that day, 16th March 2021; this was the day her dear friend was receiving her MRI results from her 19th February scan. Remember, readers, that was the day of our five-month reunion, when we'd had our perfect picnic together on the hospital car park turfed area.

The day that I went for my final results, 16th March, Martina was there at the hospital receiving yet more chemotherapy. I asked her if I could nip and see her before I heard my final news. She looked forward to me popping to her bedside to see her. I could not have walked the same ground as her without visiting the chemo bays. There was no way I could miss the small chance of her being awake and smiling back at me for a few minutes. I turned up to see her, but she wasn't awake. My heart sank — such a missed opportunity to be with my dear sister. I could see her in the corner bed, out of my reach and too ill for me to disturb her sleep. I felt robbed of her beautiful soul as she lay there in the chemo ward with a drip in her hand. This was only about fifteen minutes before I received the "all clear" news. With a heavy heart from seeing her sleeping, I re-joined the oncology outpatients department where Richard was waiting for me.

I am here, able to write this book, so you all know that I received brilliant news!

The time had come to call my dear Martina and tell her my brilliant outcome. I called her an hour and a half later after visiting her when she was sleeping in the chemo ward.

She was awake now and longed for my news. This makes my eyes well up as I write this part because that would have been so tough on her, to hear I had no cancer, but she was waiting for my phone call with regard to my results. Again, a cruel blow for her was that it was her chemo day when I shared my great news with her. How very unfair, I thought! My husband drove us back from Derby Hospital, and I sat in the passenger seat as I released tears of relief to my in-laws. Then came the call to Martina. My heart sank as I dialled her number. As the words poured from my lips that I was cancer-free, I broke down in tears to Martina. This was the sharpest twist of the knife for our sistership — I was sharing my "living on" news with my precious sister while she was dying! I ended the call so unhappy for her; I felt helpless and desperate about her situation. We were going to be parted, and we knew it. I hated cancer so much for doing this to us both. It had one sister in its clutches and one sister that it had let escape.

As she heard my wonderful news, her voice was filled with happiness and love. I can hear her voice now. At this very moment tears are flowing down my cheeks as I write this. This is so tough to share.

She replied, "Michelle, I am so, so happy for you. Michelle, same boat, different direction." What an amazing soul to have reacted in this way. She also said, "Go home and have lots of chilled bubbly. Party hard tonight, hey?" I ended the call in bits; I was gutted for her and her tiny tight-knit family.

Such a mix of emotions was flooding from my heart, one half filled with absolute joy and relief and one half torn out and terrified that my friend was dying. For the next week or so, I was manic. I wanted to save my dear friend from death. I felt so useless, unhappy, tearful and down in the dumps every time she crossed my mind.

My Martina, engraved in my heart like battle lines of a tree trunk. Every few minutes that passed, I would think of her. I would stand and wash the pots and think of her. I would do gardening and think of her. I would drive to and fro and think of her. She was — and is — every heartbeat of me.

Looking Back

I lost all of my hair, and I mean ALL the hair: smooth legs, smooth armpits, and no pubic hair for months and months. No shaving — it was brilliant! I lost some eyelashes, but they returned in three weeks. I was amazed by this.

I stopped drinking alcohol and having treats. I did all I could to live a "clean" lifestyle. Instead of chocolate and cake, I ate peppers, nuts and fruits. I took turmeric supplements throughout my chemotherapy and radiotherapy treatments. When these twelve weeks came to an end, I took olive leaf supplements and vitamin D supplements. Did these help my body? Yes, I'm sure of it. Supplements, I believe, boost the immune system. I am still taking them to this day.

I felt absolutely amazing — not ill at all. The only way you could tell that I was a cancer victim was that I had no hair. Friends who were aware of my diagnosis all said that they couldn't believe how well I looked. I am still unsure to this day how I could feel so well and be carrying late-stage cancer around in my body. It was totally nuts! During every treatment I was glowing! I had realised I had to grab every second of every day and be the very best me whilst doing so.

Nothing changed home-wise: all was normal. I was floating around, happy and bubbly, make-up looking great, my slim body functioning as usual. I was hoovering up, cooking the teatime meals, sitting out in the sunshine — nothing seemed dangerous. At night-times though, that's when my mind raced with fear if I wasn't busy.

Six weeks in, the hair was now falling out at a rapid pace, and the wig and chiffon floral bows were now starting to make their daily appearances. It was a harsh reality — now I did feel like a cancer patient as I had the resounding evidence: my bald appearance! The frightening reminder of death that I couldn't always hide, my loss of hair, was the whistle blower that my body was being poisoned and that the cancer was trying to kill me. It was a race to see who would survive — me or the cancer.

I'd look in the mirror and think, "My poor kids and husband! Look at what an ugly mess my scalp looks!" I tried to cover my bald head as much as I could for their sakes. It was summer now though, and the wig was too hot to wander round in — thank goodness that I had many scarves that I had built up over the years due to loving wearing them with outfits.

When I learnt of my cancer, my wardrobe was already well stocked for head coverings. These weren't just a box of scarves anymore that made my blazers look smart — overnight, each and every scarf turned into my identity; these flimsy feminine pieces of material were now Michelle. The plastic box of many patterns and colours instantly offered me beauty and confidence. The chiffon bow was now the new me, the new mum and wife that appeared every morning out from the bedroom door, swanning into the kitchen with my perfectly styled bow on board and my bold new make-up style. The daily morning double feelgood factor of my bow and make-up uplifted me and handed my heart the fabulous boost it needed to face each day.

When I lost the hair, it was easier to practise the bows. When I had hair, my hair would get in the way of tying the bow; this was annoying as it was stopping me from having the perfect bow. God, I loved my beautiful bow, it was my saviour.

Again, time-wise, this was around the time I started having to dash into the back bedroom or garden if people we knew came to our door. My husband's BMX business meant that people were knocking on our front door in the afternoons. I'd see them approaching and think, "Oh shit!" and I would have to run through the living room and dining room area of the house in a panicked state in order to call my husband from the top of our garden, where he'd be working.

I would be squawking Richard's name to come and sort out these threats at my door, and Richard would come running to my rescue. I wasn't going to show these visitors my cancer bow. It looked beautiful but screamed illness!

Fast forward a few months and New Year's Eve was upon us. Myself and my daughter made memories. I got tipsy on two gins; I had barely consumed any alcohol since July. My daughter and I agreed to get really dressed up and we danced around the living room. It was a right laugh; I think us two giggling the night away got on my husband's nerves slightly — sorry, Richard!

Richard and I retired to our bedroom. We laid in bed and watched Big Ben on TV. It was lovely and cosy, and I embraced

Richard in a tipsy state. I hoped this wouldn't be the last New Year's Eve that I cuddled him. This was the thought that ran through my mind as the celebrations were shown on TV. As I heard Big Ben chime out the terrible year that we'd been experiencing and bring in the new one, I hoped to God that the treatment had worked its magic on me. I held Richard tight and kissed him. My goodness, it had been a scary 2020. Would 2021 bring great joy and hope? I was crossing every bone in my body that the cancer was no longer alive. I prayed that the cancer demon had been annihilated. My wish came true — such joy! The ultimate gift was handed to me.

Cervical Cancer

S o, cervical cancer. As a survivor of this cancer, I am now very clued up on this disease, but until cancer appeared I did not know much about it. As women, we know that we should go for smear tests, and that is what I did, but many women don't attend their appointments as they feel it is embarrassing and not a pleasant thing to willingly subject themselves to.

What do we get so worked up about though? It's a two-minute check. We are all born through the cervix if you've been delivered by natural measures. Half of our DNA has passed through the cervix to create life. Yet it seems such a taboo to talk about this body part.

As soon as we become sexually active as young adults, we subject ourselves to a virus called HPV, contracted through sexual activity. This virus can survive in our bodies for many years — silently, with no symptoms. Our body usually fights off this virus. This virus, HPV, causes abnormal cells to grow on the cervix. HPV stands for Human Papilloma Virus. When you go for a cervical screening check-up (smear), HPV can be detected on the smear test slide sample in the laboratory.

Ladies who have abnormalities on their cervix (that are detected by a GP or a smear sample in a lab) are referred to have a colposcopy check at the Gynaecology department at their local hospital — this is a camera that looks at the cervix. Abnormalities are usually referred to as pre-cancerous cells.

Abnormal cells can usually be removed by different methods. When you go for a colposcopy appointment, if the medical staff are unsure of what they are dealing with, this is when a biopsy may be taken from the cervix to check for cancer cells; this is what happened to me. Going for your smear test is vitally important — spotting abnormalities early before they turn into cancer is what the aim of the smear test is all about. Cancer can happen between smears — this is less common, but it is possible. This is what happened in my case. HPV took a really good hold on my cervix during the three-year period between my smear check-ups, and by the time I attended my 2020 smear test, the abnormalities had turned into aggressive cancer. My bad luck was now life-threatening!

I was due my smear check-up in December 2019 but because I had my period I went for the screening in very early January 2020. Late-stage cancer wasn't spotted on my sample. Cervical screening looks for HPV and abnormalities.

Every woman who is rocked by cervical cancer has her screening history reviewed. This looks for evidence of error. I was very unlucky! My cancer occurred between 2016 and 2020 — the hospital informed me of this at my review and I have a letter stating this (which I framed, believe it or not!)

HPV is a viral infection transmitted by skin-to-skin contact, so there you go — as soon as you sleep with someone unprotected, you open yourself up to the HPV virus. This causes over 90% of cervical cancer cases. There are around 13 very dangerous strains of HPV and if one of these shows up on your smear slide, you will get called back every year for a smear test so that the hospital can monitor any cervical changes. There are over a hundred strains of HPV, but around 13 of these are deemed very troublesome and, if left untreated, cervical cancer could happen. It is vital at any age to attend your appointments. As I have mentioned, HPV is something you can carry as soon as you are sexually active.

I was in my mid-forties when HPV became a danger to my health. Bear in mind, I've been happily married and faithful for 21 years. The HPV would have just been sitting dormant in my body and I was totally clueless of its threat to my life. It is scary, but that is why ladies must go for their smear check-ups so that medical staff can detect subtle changes that we are blissfully unaware of inside our cervix.

Please go for your smear tests, ladies. I'm of the mind that if you can afford a yearly private screening for cervical cancer, this would be money well spent.

The Best Day Of My Life

H ere it was, the day I had longed for, the day I would know if I was well again. 16th March 2021; it was a Tuesday. I'd been for my final MRI on 19th February 2021 to see how the treatment had affected my cancer. I then had to wait to see my oncologist on 16th March 2021 at 3 p.m. to receive my final news. I was scared. The almost four-week time span between the MRI and the news day was a very lengthy wait, but someone had informed me that if the MRI was showing cancer then somebody would get in touch with me sooner.

This was challenging, as every time my phone rang over that four-week period my heart was in my mouth thinking the hospital was calling me to tell me bad news. I would look at my phone screen and be so happy that it was not showing a Derby area code. Even though I didn't get a call, I couldn't let myself think I was cancer-free until I heard it from a professional's lips.

On this day in question there were so many people wanting to know the outcome that I decided to write a list of names that I would move through if the news was good. I was desperate to cross these names out with happiness with a huge fat marker pen. My mind was imagining how fabulous this moment would feel, telling all who loved me that I was free of my biggest ever problem!

I got smartly dressed. My tummy was churning; my mind was numb. I can't get carried away yet, I thought. I had no gut feeling. My body had felt this good last year and I'd had cancer and didn't know it! We left the house at 2 p.m. The beast, my friend, came with us to hold my hand; it delivered us safely to the hospital. I was a bag of nerves, dreading the worst. What news were they going to break to me? It seemed to take forever to drive there.

Richard and I walked into the hospital and checked in. Previous to this checking in, I had nipped to see my darling sister Martina. It was now 2.30 p.m. We took a seat and waited. 3 p.m. was soon upon us. My tummy was like a tumble dryer; wow, my stomach was in knots. Finally, I heard the words "Michelle Camm". Here we go, I thought. My heart was in my mouth. My husband and I walked into the room where the oncologist sat looking at us, Richard and I gripping each other's hands.

"Okay, Mrs Camm," he said, "your MRI is showing no cancer." Boom! Bloody hell, I couldn't believe it. I was totally stunned. I sat, not smiling, not laughing. I was just in sheer shock, sheer disbelief that the treatment had worked for me, that my body had responded so brilliantly to it. I was proud; so proud that I'd done all I could to help my body. I'd drunk so much horrid green tea. I'd tried to just be me; to be positive. It had worked! Everything must have worked alongside each other, all working like a well-oiled engine.

"Sorry, so again," I heard my husband ask, "there's no cancer on my wife's MRI?"

"That's correct," the doctor replied. I turned to my husband, looked into his eyes and cheekily pulled down his mask and mine too — we were wearing masks because of the Covid pandemic — and I stole a kiss of celebration, one small but joyous peck, then replaced our masks. His eyes were filled with joy and love. We had done it; we had worked through the cancer.

He was my rock. The strongest I could ever wish for, the strongest I'd ever known him. This was a battle we'd won together. Cancer happens in one person but drags the whole family in. My two teenage children are rocks too. I'm one lucky lady. They were there, my husband and children — they had stopped the fierce ocean from taking me.

As we walked out of the room where we'd been told no cancer was showing, we proceeded down the corridor towards the exit of the hospital. Holding hands, we were stunned, hardly saying anything to each other. We were in total shock. My eyes started to well up. We had a huge hug and we walked towards the exit again. We were heading down the corridor to where I had received radiotherapy. This was on the basement level of the hospital.

I had it on my mind that I must not forget to ring the bell — the cancer bell. Don't forget to ring the bell, I kept thinking to myself. Many bells are located in different parts of the hospital. All the cancer treatment wards I have visited have a bell so that patients can celebrate and mark the end of their treatment. When I ended my treatments, all three times, I did not once have the desire to ring the bell. I felt like it was tempting fate.

As we walked towards the exit doors of the hospital, the

radiotherapy bell was the closest one to use. We made our way to this level by walking down three flights of stairs. These stairs I had used many times but never with these butterflies in my tummy and multi-coloured unicorns in my head. Flipping heck, I wanted to run down those stairs. I wanted to jump on the hand-rail and slide my way to the very bottom. I was on top of the world! I couldn't get down there quick enough to grab hold of that rope and make the bell ring out loud. The ringing of celebration was now mine for the taking! I was now free again to smile wholeheartedly. Free of my demon. Free of my fear. Free to smile without worry. This I hadn't been truly capable of for nine months.

I had waited so long for this joyous moment. I had waited so long for my chance to arrive, to hold the rope attached to this dream bell. It had been five months since my last treatment. I was brimming with enthusiasm to get down those steps, stand next to the big silver wall-mounted bell, smash the insides of the bell with the inner rope and ding-a-ling it with passion and freedom.

We reached the reception desk, and I asked their permission to ring the bell. The ladies at reception replied, "Of course you can."

I rang it so hard and true. It was a tremendous celebration, and I just couldn't believe that I was ringing it. What it actually represented to grab hold of the rope was stupendous. My husband videoed every second of my momentous milestone, and had to tell me to stop ringing it, the ladies behind the desk clapping as I rang it and laughing at my husband's comment. I approached the desk and told them how I hadn't wanted to engage in the bell ringing unless I received cancer-free news. This video is one that I could watch over and over again; I will never tire of watching it.

What a fantastic day it was. To be told I was cancer-free; to ring the bell; to call my children; to walk out of hospital and cry tears of relief and joy with my husband by my side; to run around my village spreading my happy news to my neighbours; to share this news with my close family and friends. Wow, wow, wow — it was the most special day of my life.

It felt bloody awesome to be told that no cancer was showing on my MRI, and tears of happiness and disbelief were rolling down my face as we headed to our car. Even the weather was stunning. It was a beautiful spring afternoon, and the sunshine was celebrating with us, throwing its bright rays down on us like golden confetti. "Take that!" it was saying. The heat of the sun felt like a big pair of hands had reached into a joyous box of sparkly messy particles and was letting them loose on my head. My husband gripped my hand so tightly. We were in shock; it was thrilling. We just did not know what to do or say; we were just in fairy-tale land on hearing the super news. There will never be a day like it again, I hope, but that day was so, so special. To be told that my life wasn't hanging in the balance was indescribable. It took weeks to stop buzzing from it.

As we walked towards the car park, it dawned on me; I could share this fabulous news with my children. I called my son first because I'd told him that I'd be calling him around 3.30 p.m., but because I'd remembered to ring the bell, we were a little later out of hospital than I'd planned. He picked up. "I'm okay," I said. "They can't see any cancer." The best ever news that I could deliver down the handset to him. "They say no cancer can be detected on the MRI that I had in February," I said. My son made me repeat what I had said; he was also in total shock at what I was informing him of. I repeated my fabulous news; tears were streaming down my face. My hubby and I at this point had reached a pedestrian crossing. People, total strangers, could hear me speaking on my mobile. It felt brilliant, and I felt so proud to speak these words. As I walked and talked and clasped Richard's hand so tightly in happiness, thoughts leapt through my mind that my scary test was at its finish line.

I didn't care that folk could hear me. It was the best news ever! I'd been handed life — what could beat that?

It was amazing to say those words to Owen. Telling my son that I was safe and well, that his mum wasn't going to die! Can you imagine how special and euphoric that was for me to be in that bubble, to live that moment?

Next, I called my daughter. She didn't pick up, so I called again, and this time she picked up. "I'm okay, I'm okay! I have no cancer showing on my MRI!" I repeated. My daughter started to cry down the phone, which tugged at my heartstrings. I was well again — how bloody awesome! It was another superb moment, telling her that I was okay and that treatment had worked. Sharing with my daughter that her very best friend, her shopping pal, her female confidante wasn't going to leave her side and leave her life at such a young age, that she could just carry on confiding in the mum she cared for and relied upon so much. It was just spectacular to give this gift to my two children on that day.

Such wonderful phone calls they were. The best ones I will ever make. I'll hold those two calls so dear until I go to my grave. I will never make phone calls of joy like that ever again, I hope, to anybody.

To tell my kids that I was safe, there are no words for this. In the space of a few minutes, I changed their world. I gave them the gift of life all over again that day, but the difference was that there wasn't a birthday attached to it. It was MY second birthday, my chance to relive and my chance to carry on being their mum.

We arrived back home, and I flung my arms around my daughter. My son wasn't home from work yet. My daughter and I broke down in tears, cuddling each other. I kissed her soft brown hair and tears streamed with relief. We giggled and said how wonderful it was; what a special precious mark on our lives that moment was. It was a never to be repeated feeling, I hope. The cancer cloud had lifted from our beautiful cottage; we could start enjoying our days again without the heavy worry.

Such special, miraculous, happy news — nothing I ever experience again will be as special as that day.

In the afternoon we were in raptures; we couldn't believe that the treatment had worked. It was madness. It was like a "What now?" feeling, like it had been a big trick; it felt very weird, as if we were stunned and lost in a maze.

That night my daughter went out, my son went fishing, and my husband went upstairs for a bath. It was so strange; so quiet. I sat on the sofa with my hand on our dog's back. She was snoring away. It felt so normal, so peaceful and carefree, just like life before cancer. I decided to message my neighbours. It was dark and cold, and I had my PJs on. I asked Emma, Diana and Emily if they were up for a celebration. "Are you coming out in the dark on the green for a glass of bubbly?" I asked. Emma was unable to join due to work commitments, but the others agreed. We sat on the bench in the pitch black drinking Asti from crystal flute glasses. To be honest, we sat behind a holly bush, because we were a group of three and at that time the Covid guidelines only allowed meeting up with one other person, so it meant our little group had to hide and keep quiet. However, I'd just got the news that I was cancer-free — I think I at least deserved a small gathering in the dark outside. We had my speaker on low playing dance music, and we sat eating orange Matchmakers and mint Aero — it was brilliant! I had my faux fur coat on over my PJs and my neighbours laughed at me. I didn't care; I was free.

It felt great. We sat out for about an hour. It was cold. But it was just so, so wonderful to do that — to have my own little private party to celebrate not having cancer. It was unforgettable to share that day's news in the evening with my closest village friends. They had supported me bucket loads and they'd given me top-dollar friendship. I can never thank them enough.

We couldn't even go out to celebrate as everything was closed due to Covid restrictions. I didn't care a hoot though; I didn't need a pub or restaurant to make me smile or feel special. I was floating on cloud nine.

Twelve hours on from hearing the thrilling life-changing news and after only being asleep in my bed for four solid hours, I woke. What was happening to me was magical and real. The next decision changed my life.

My brain was buzzing; it felt like Christmas Day but a hundred times more thrilling. My healthy body enjoyed the pleasure of the soft mattress; every inch of my being was overwhelmed.

I carefully snuck out of bed so that my husband wouldn't be disturbed, and I wandered into the living room. I rested every inch of my relieved body and soul in the still empty chair that had beckoned me to a corner of my cosy front room. My goodness, this morning in question was such a stark contrast to all the other very early mornings that I had been woken. These had been caused by an immense fear of failure of treatment, maybe even death! The very same chair had always comforted me, though this morning was like no other that I had felt before — it was enchanting; it was the highest level of elation and disbelief. I had won life — what vocabulary is there to describe that?

Hundreds of previous early mornings had seen me wallowing in this very same chair. Here I now sat and shared my delight — my cancer story — on Facebook. The post was popular; it struck a chord not only with my friends but with strangers too. This really was quite surprising to be honest, and the love and support felt very humbling. I was on a total high from the response of the Facebook post, which made me realise that I wanted to do so much more to help raise awareness of cervical cancer. I was bouncing with joy; no feeling could ever compare to somebody telling you that you are not going to die. The worry and fear had been swept away from family life — it was totally superb. Every minute of the day was fabulous. I was elated because the brilliant news had impacted on my friends' lives too; the weight of my poor health on their shoulders was now something that they could stop fretting about.

The dog was snoring away and the clock was ticking on the dining room wall. I sat on the living room recliner, just stunned. I picked up my mobile phone and wrote a heartfelt unplanned post on Facebook. The emotion was raw; my journey, my fear, came spilling out as my fingertips typed a brief write-up. My purpose, as I typed, was for just one lady to read my post and go for her overdue smear test. At this point I wasn't even 100% sure that I was going to press "Post"; I was just writing my feelings down.

I read over what I had typed. I thought, even if just a dozen people share it, maybe a few women will take note of my hell and wake up and smell the coffee. So I did it: I hit "Post". I was proud to post it. I wanted some positive to come from my hell.

Little did I know what mayhem this would stir. It was wonderful. I never in a million years did it for attention — it was purely for women's health. My phone was bonkers for three days plus. Messages, well wishes, strangers commenting on my post — it was brilliant! This, on top of the news I'd had the day before, was truly mind-blowing. I couldn't leave my phone alone; there were so many messages to read and respond to. I was touched by people's kindness. The post was shared more than 300 times just from what I could see. I will never know the overall figures, I'm afraid. That will remain Facebook's secret.

After posting my Facebook post early on Wednesday morning at around 4 a.m., I decided at 10 a.m. the same day while I was at work to also put the same post on my business page for my customers. I thought it would be wonderful to say thank you to them because their custom had kept my heart and head afloat.

It felt fabulous as I posted the story. I had a lot to thank my customers for — their clothing orders had kept my life normal, kept me from overthinking what might be ahead. Their response was humbling. Customers were very shocked that I'd had cancer; they were totally unaware of what I had been contending with. I'd been able to steam ahead and keep my brain busy whilst still being well enough to attend work. By 26th March 2021, the post had reached 8,000 readers. A great platform for spreading awareness! I was really pleased with the outcome.

My customers didn't see me for nine months, you see. If there were any orders to personally hand out, I would send my husband, as my cancer bow would have given the game away that I was ill. Richard, my husband, would play along with our well-hatched plan and say I was too busy to meet customers. Richard was the main face of the business for nine months whilst I couldn't face regular friendly customers. So that's how we kept my illness from everyone — teamwork prevailed yet again.

I'm going to add this into the story because it's important to me. When I shared my story on Facebook, it ran through my mind that some readers wouldn't fully read my post and think, "Stupid woman for not keeping up to date with cervical screening check-ups". It crossed my mind for a few seconds that people might think bad of me, even though I had been for regular screening and my cancer had taken hold between the 2016 and early 2020 smears.

I pressed post anyway, because I wanted to raise awareness. I didn't care if people thought bad of me; I just wanted to inform women, dads and boyfriends and for them to talk about my post. That was my ONLY aim.

Spreading my story early that morning not only raised awareness, it also brought back a dear friend to me. We fell out two years ago over something so stupid. She saw my story and got back in touch with me saying she was sobbing her heart out that she hadn't been there for me. This was the evening of 17th March. I was just so happy that she had found the courage to message me. Cancer has showered me with so many special relationships that I didn't expect but truly treasure. She is my friend Alisha. When we were friends, it was such a wonderful part of my life. I loved her like a sister. She and her husband would come to our house for tea in the evenings. They were really great friends of ours, and then it all got spoilt because of a feud.

It cut really deep when she left my life; she had been a very valued friend for a good few years. Another friendship where we just clicked. On Saturday 26th March 2021 she came up to my village and it was like no fallout had even happened. Her beautiful smile greeted me from the passenger seat of her car as she sat putting on her walking boots. It was amazing to be in her presence again. We planned to meet again at the end of that week. A few nights after her first message, we spent two hours on Messenger — madness I know, but the years I'd missed were like a drug; I just couldn't stop talking to her and it was likewise for Alisha too.

That day was a wonderful day. We walked and talked and ate chips out of their wrapper that we bought from a small local chippy in Kimberley. We laughed, smiled and totally sucked up each other's auras. We'd had two years apart, but it felt like only a week had passed since seeing her last. A great, great day. Thank you, cancer, for giving my friend a reason to get back in touch with me.

A Whirlwind Of Emotions

It was 11 a.m. on 17th March, less than 24 hours on from receiving the good news from the hospital, and I didn't have much clothing printing to complete at work. I asked my husband if he minded me returning home as I wanted to walk in the sunshine. It was a beautiful sunny day; the morning was fabulous. I had been up since 3.30 a.m. as this was when I had decided to let loose on social media that I had been battling cancer. Facebook was going mad with well wishes from people. That day I carried a grin like a Cheshire cat, but emotions would soon turn the opposite way for my heart.

I decided on my walk back that I wanted to help other ladies in my position. I wanted to share my experience and provide support if women needed it. I hated the thought of other ladies having those really dark moments that I'd had in those very first few weeks after receiving the devastating news. I imagined distraught, broken-hearted, desperate women in the same lonely scenario that I had also been in.

I emailed Gynaecology and they called me back within 30 minutes. They thought it was fabulous that I wanted to help. I'm not sure they believed I would follow it through though, as it was only 24 hours from receiving my news. I think they thought that when the dust had settled, I might change my mind on offering up my help. I wasn't going to — I was on a mission to save ladies' lives.

After calling Gynaecology with my offer, they invited me in to listen to some ideas of mine; ways in which they could improve patients' experiences within the Royal Derby Hospital. I have said that they can use me however possible in the future, as I am a walking example that serious late-stage patients do get a second chance at health.

This day was totally mind-blowing. I had been told I had no cancer showing the day previous after worrying for nine months about it. My phone was electric with people and friends who were over the moon for me. My brain was firing on all cylinders. It was totally spectacular.

Wednesday lunchtime arrived. Now I was in floods of tears from relief and the chance of more life to come. It felt like I'd won millions of pounds. My heart was singing.

All of the above emotions lasted weeks, they truly did. I wish I could have bottled the positive feelings to be able to return to the bottle and take the lid off for more of those tingles. It was like an addiction — it was total ecstasy! But around this wonderful sunshine of joy was a cloud of sadness for my dear friend Martina. I could not shake the worry and fear. It was as though the percentage sat at 60% sunshine and 40% grey misery.

My diary entry for 17th March 2021 stated: "I know that Martina has a much heavier burden to contend with — death. It is a billion times worse for her, but I feel so helpless that I just have to watch and wait for her to disappear from my life. I feel I am letting her down, but I can offer nothing to make her whole again, apart from our deep bond of friendship that she appreciates so much. She wants to know all about my days, what I am up to, but I feel cruel sharing my brilliant times with her. I have spoken to her about this, but she is just happy to hear what I have been up to.

"Her days are slow and sleepy and full of pain; she looks forward to these chapters that I read to her. I write the stories and she loves to hear my voice sharing the many things that are unfolding for me. It makes me feel like a monster when I tell her of my days. It makes me feel like I am rubbing salt in her wounds. I have spoken at great length with her about these emotions that I have when I tell her of my thrilling days, but she reassures me that she looks forward to hearing what crazy experiences are landing at my feet. She says she is happy to hear of my adventures.

"Martina's suffering hurts me so much; my heart is so heavy with worry and dread for her. Tough as this is, I will never forget the bond we have created together in the seven short months that we have been close. She has been my golden angel through my journey. I write these stories daily, and in the evenings, when my brain and heart can't cope with the abundance of emotions I'm having to process. I feel I am grieving for Martina before it has even happened.

"The funny, happy stories I do write, I read to Martina by WhatsApp voice message. She tells me she likes to save them until night-time to listen to them. It's like her little treat, she says. I think this is lovely. She has a dot of happiness to focus on, so I carry on sending her my many stories. My family wonder why I am so emotional and down, but it's Martina. The worry of not having her in my life takes over the fact that cancer is no longer showing in my body.

"All the stories I send Martina she loves. I ask her, "Are they book-worthy?" She replies, "Yes." I just can't imagine life without her; it's going to be like losing an arm when cancer finally claims her.

"I'm very tearful a lot of the time, it's all too much to cope with. These emotions swirling around me are from the happiness of being well again, the thought of me losing my closest dearest friend, the weird gap that cancer has left in my daily life and the fear that cancer may regrow in the period of time that the hospital is not monitoring me over the next six months. There is little advice when you receive this brilliant news that you don't have cancer showing. That sounds like a strange request, but it really does leave a huge question mark of how to move forward and revert back to normal life. Now I have a six-month wait until I have another MRI to see if cancer has stayed away. The worry doesn't totally go away. Cancer could haunt me again — this is something that I have to live with. Aggressive cancer is more likely to reappear. These are my daily thoughts that loom in the very back of my mind."

Four days on. It was the Saturday that followed Tuesday's great news. I felt a bit steadier with my emotions. I have a mirrored wardrobe in the corner of my bedroom with double doors. On receiving my treatment plan, way back in the July of 2020, I'd gone to my make-up drawer and chosen a bright red lipstick. On the left-side mirror door, I'd made a stick chart of all my treatments that were to come. At the very top of the door were six lines, and I'd crossed one line out every Tuesday evening after attending my chemo session. It felt liberating crossing each week off. Looking at the mirror with the marks being destroyed was very satisfying.

Under the six lines that I'd drawn, there were also marks that stated W1 through to W6. W1 represented week 1 of radiotherapy, and within that week I had also received a stronger dose of chemo than in the previous six weeks. So, in a nutshell, W1 was a dose of radiotherapy every day and the seventh week of chemotherapy. It was a sure way of staying focussed and seeing the progress that I was making.

Every Friday evening there was a glimmer of positivity. I could reach for my red lipstick and cross off another treatment week that started with a W. It was like a weight being lifted from my shoulders; it was therapy for my mind and my worried heart. Drawing a line of relief through the stick chart that I had created meant I was another week closer to ending the travelling, poison and radiation. The word BRACHY marked the very last treatment. Bloody hell, I dreaded this word that I'd written in red lipstick. This was the radiotherapy delivered internally into my cervix.

When I crossed through the word BRACHY, this was the most awesome feeling ever. This was at the very end of September. I was home, sore and stiff from being in bed for 34 hours, but I didn't care — that was my very last treatment over and done with, totally finished, the absolute END. I hoped I would never have to have cancer treatment again in my life!

Now it was 20th March, four days on from knowing I was well again, and I was more than ready to say goodbye to the lipstick chart that I had been staring at for nine months with dread, hope and anticipation. Where is that F**KING glass cleaner, I thought. Yes, it was time to claim my full-length left wardrobe mirrored door back, to clean it free of the evil marks of my fright. I was itching to get rid of the horrible reminder that I'd looked at every day when getting dressed. Every day when I picked out my nice clothes, there were the marks reminding me of all that I had been through, of all the procedures my super body had had to absorb. The marks had been there from July 2020 to March 2021. I couldn't wait to wipe them away — what they represented was the scariest thing I've ever had to face.

"Can you video me cleaning away my chart, please?" I said to Richard. He replied, "Yes mate." He stood videoing me as I prepared to clean the lipstick away with glass cleaner.

I said to my husband, "Are you ready?" My glass cleaner gun in my hand, my heart filled with butterflies of happiness. "Yes," he said. I sprayed the glass cleaner all over the crossed-off lipstick marks on the door. Bloody hell, it felt fantastic; it felt like a rebirth. I wiped away the lipstick; I wiped away the dread. I yelped, "Yes! Yes!" and I flung my arms in the air in celebration that the marks were gone and what it represented for the marks to not be visible on my wardrobe door anymore!

My, I was beaming, and celebrated with such pleasure. It was a truly remarkable moment and one that I'll never forget. A wonderful video to watch. My arms were so high above my head as I grabbed the glass cleaner in one hand and a flannel in the other, my arms cheering to say, "It's over, it's gone! Yay!" It felt mint. I was smiling and giggling and so wonderfully happy. Wow, when I watch it back, it's fantastic to relive that moment; to see the relief on my face.

Tears To Treasure

I t was 10 a.m. on Saturday 20th March. Only about an hour had passed since the red lipstick marks story. I was still deep in a euphoric state due to all the attention and excitement that was being thrown at my feet. I had undertaken a massive journey and now I was at my most longed-for destination. I was back to normal health!

My son walked downstairs and asked if I could take him to the local retail park to meet his girlfriend of three years. I agreed to help him. I told him to grab my car keys and I would get my shoes and bag. He waited for me in the front passenger seat of my cherished beast, my Honda. It was a stunning day. The beautiful March spring morning filled my heart; the sun was divine as it peaked through the perfect fluffy clouds, and the sky was so still — it was clear blue glory.

I started my engine by pressing in the start button, then opened up the huge glass sunroof to take advantage of the beaming hot sun. It flooded in through the roof of my car. My face was graced with a humble grin; I felt so privileged to be well again and to be able to do such a simple favour for my son without worry.

My son remarked, "Mum, what are you doing opening the

sunroof? It's only March!" I replied in the most upbeat manner, "Let in the sunshine — life is great!" I waved my hands to beckon in the sunlight. He laughed at me. I was so high on life, and it felt marvellous.

I drove to the retail park that was only a five-minute drive away. I waved my son goodbye. Down my foot went on the gas pedal; I could tell the turbo wanted to play! My smile was so obvious to all who glanced at me driving along. I was soaking up how incredible the news had been. The cancer had been devoured by the treatment. My heart was filled with contentment.

I turned down the country lane that leads to our village. There was nobody on the lane that day, and I took advantage of the country lane. The speedometer read 45 mph; it felt superb. Each second that passed, I felt as if it was raining money. Round the bends I slowed right down, moving through the gears of my beast. The sun was still blazing through the sunroof onto my now pixie-length hairstyle, and the radio was playing 1990s dance music. Gosh, it was incredible!

I thought, "Oh my goodness, what a car — what a piece of super sexy engineering!" I slowed right down as I moved towards our village. I was now letting the emotion flood out. The corners are quite nasty and blind, so I crept along the tarmac. A song was playing on the radio that I adored, and my voice was singing out so loud. I held the tiny, sporty steering wheel and let the flared bonnet and my beautiful friend return us into the village, where the sight of our pretty cottages blessed my eyes.

My car crawled along our unadopted village road, over two speed humps and up to where my daughter parks her car. A little further than this sat Emma's driveway. My face was now wet through with tears that were rolling down my cheeks. I had to share this overwhelming moment and my zest for life with my wonderful rock, Emma.

The displays of emotion that I was now consumed by had been negligible throughout our daily walks we had shared together over the many months. I thought it so poignant for her to witness my significant display of relief. As I drove my car nearer to her house it became so apparent to me how much I had needed her friendship, her love and her willingness to give me unconditional support. How grateful I was that she had been by my side every step of the way. I abandoned my car at the end of Emma's drive and ran to her door, grabbing the huge old-fashioned door knocker. There I stood, waiting for my beloved friend to answer, needing to show her my gratitude and elation. She came very swiftly to the door. "What's happened, my love?" she asked. "I'm just so happy that you have helped me through my cancer," I replied, and I went on to say how I wanted her to share in my extreme joy and how much I had appreciated her friendship.

"Oh, my love," she said, and flung her arms around me. She gave me the biggest loving hug. I was in a right state. We went and sat on her front bench, and we were both so thrilled about my heath. I looked down at her pale blue sweat jumper, covered in my snot and tears from my snivelling episode at her door. I remarked, "That's a true friend, that is — you have my snot and tears all over your jumper." We laughed hard. She replied, "I don't mind."

Emma, this is another memory I will take to my grave. You are such a wonderful person.

Dear Diary

30th March 2021.

Two weeks since hearing the "no cancer" comment spill from my doctor's lips. I can't believe where the days have gone. It is now Monday 11 a.m., two weeks exactly from finding out that my body is free of my demon. I just about feel back to normal now; the excitement has almost worn off. My brain no longer feels as if it's a Rolodex. As though it's being controlled by a ghost, flicking through the many cards of information at a pace of a thousand miles an hour.

Writing in my diary really has been so helpful; this £1 diary purchase is the reason I can tell you all of my fight, my loss, my loves and my achievements. It has slowed me down and made me sit; let my mind ponder and process. It forces me to chill. As I write this, tears stream down my face. Such simple stories will hopefully help many hearts. The ticking clock, my old trusty friend, has witnessed all of my emotions, but mainly bad ones over these many months. That clock, it must think that I'm a right misery guts! Now it sits high on the dining room wall telling me that I can enjoy life once again. There's just a balloon swaying in the dining room. This is the only movement happening in the house at the moment. The balloon was a gift that my daughter bought for me one day after my brilliant news. It is royal blue with the word "Congratulations" written across it. My daughter, bless her, appeared from a card shop and walked over to my car with it in her hand. How thoughtful of her!

I have been awake only half an hour. What a solid sleep I have had! Cancer is now off my mind, and I am sleeping like a log. I opened my bedroom curtains and there it was — bright yellow sunshine! My beautiful garden filled my heart and mind with pleasure once again. Two hundred yellow zingy daffodils are all over my garden, swaying in the breeze. Their brightness is their celebration for me; do they know my outcome, I wonder? It's a picture; I planted those bulbs not knowing if I would see them bloom, back in the October of 2020.

Every bulb I touched, I was hoping that I would be well enough to get up close and bend down to sniff the trumpet middles, and not be lying in my bed dying from this terrible disease. As I planted them in pots and in the ground, I really had no clue how the treatment had affected my body. I was thinking, as I touched each bulb, "Will these daffodils be waving me out of this world whilst the wind gently rocks them in the soil?"

Our bedroom is on the ground floor of our tiny cottage, and French doors lead out onto the small, gravelled courtyard. This is covered in fine gravel, which is a golden colour. Up three sleeper steps you climb and onto the lawn you arrive: my paradise, my hobby, my gym. This area, my garden, made me fit and strong, and prepared my body to fight cancer. I owe so much to my wonderful garden, but just for today I will soak up the 200 beautiful yellow daffodils and the many multi-coloured primroses that I can see, shouting "Morning, Michelle!" confidently to me. It's a great day. It's a wonderful world.

1st April 2021

It's 5 a.m., 1st April, and it is now 16 days since my news. I am awake. Once I open my eyes, I am finding it impossible to nod back off again. I am so in love with this feeling of life that I just can't settle back to sleep. It's stunning to wake up; the feeling of the excitement is like the massive bells on my alarm clock ringing out, the excitement kick-starting my mind that the day is beginning. My eyes witness the daylight shining through the bedroom curtains, and my husband's peaceful face is the loving sight that greets my eyes on these early mornings.

Richard is fast asleep next to me, and I am just so happy to lavish in watching him rest. This one thing in particular, me being able to watch him sleep, really is something I am loving the experience of doing. I am just so happy that I have more years now ahead to spend with him. There I lie, so still, watching and hearing him breathe, facing towards me. I just enjoy his closeness. I do this for a good five minutes each day when I wake up. I just appreciate Richard as he sleeps beside me.

Sixteen days have now passed, and it still feels amazing that cancer no longer burdens my mind. I am sitting on my leather sofa now, writing down my feelings. This diary is now so full, but I am glad I am keeping a record of my progress. My tummy feels like butterflies at the excitement that I'm able to live on!

The feeling that I have this morning at this early part of the day is that I've reverted back to being a child aged 8 and Christmas morning has arrived. The ultimate day of every youngster's year. When you run down the stairs and see the presents on the floor, the enchanted feeling that we all remember so well, this is the very same thrilling feeling that I have right now.

My health returning is responsible for this magical feeling. Remember when, as a child, you believed that Santa had squeezed down your chimney and left you that perfect present, all wrapped up? You have waited so long for your gift, and you hope it's what you asked Santa for on the letter that you wrote to him. It is exactly the same feeling that I have every morning. The anticipation and the wonder, the joy of this morning, is exactly comparable to that in my heart on Christmas Day 37 years ago, when I would've been only 8 years of age. Then you rip off the Christmas paper to reveal your most wanted present, the gift you so desperately desired. That is the sweet spot that I am wrapped up in right now and every morning when I open my eyes. Every day is Christmas morning to me at the moment.

14th April 2021

Today we worked up until lunch, returned home and ate our dinner in the sunny front porch, then decided to have a beautiful ride out on our fabulous friend, our motorbike, the MT-03.

We got dressed into our protective clothing and helmets, ready to make memories and have fun on the open roads of Derbyshire. We travelled from Ilkeston to Matlock then from Matlock to Bakewell then from Bakewell to Buxton. It was a very long day out, having fun and enjoying the thrills that the roads had to offer.

My joints were very stiff on arriving in Buxton, but the roads were fabulous and the pain was worth it. Richard's hands were so cold from the wind, but my hands were toasty; after all, my hands were above the exhaust, so I had no worries of icy fingertips.

As we zoomed along the A-roads I thought how beautiful a day it was and that being a biker chick is the best hobby that life offers me. The freedom, the thrills, the speed. As we rode along the winding roads and around the hairpin bends, I felt like the pendulum on a grandfather clock. We moved so smoothly together, gently rocking from side to side along the curves of the road. Being so at one with the motorbike was such a pleasure, and it just came so naturally to follow each other's body movements as we were experiencing the many lovely roads.

Just being totally relaxed and trusting my husband, at speeds that were blowing away the cobwebs and filling my heart with buckets of exhilaration. The hills and rocks we drove beneath were so black, steep and impressive. Sheep roamed the vertical rocky hills that we passed through. The sheep looked like little fluffy cotton balls, they were so high up. It was an impressive sight to witness.

The sheep roamed freely and happily all over the hillsides. I think being on a motorbike, you can really appreciate these moments so much more. You can spot ravens flying above your helmet. You have no protection around you, but this is a bonus because it means that your sight and senses have no limitations. It's just truly wonderful to have the air surrounding your body as you whizz along from place to place.

The valley we were travelling through was very low; the road was constructed between two massive hillsides. Our red motorbike looked like a ladybird crawling along the tarmac road. We passed streams and rivers — peaceful babbling waters that flowed in a sleepy manner. There were established old trees with moss-covered branches splayed over the top of the running waters. The creepy twisted branches looked like they had been covered in green luxurious velvet; it was the moss I could see but the branches looked so perfectly upholstered. The branches looked as though they were comforting the shallow waters. Nature is so stunning, even when sitting on a motorbike. Being on the motorbike seat means that there is nothing to stop your vision of nature — the wind is your 360-degree bubble as you ride along. What a perfect afternoon out! No wonder I love the bike; it offers so many unspoilt memories and sights.

Fabulous Golden Confetti

In early April the Royal Derby Hospital asked if I would be able to write a brief story of my recovery and treatments for other patients to read. This I loved doing. The staff at the RDH liked my outlook and tenacity towards cancer!

I accepted; it was going to be a total pleasure and a smidgen of payback for all the devotion and care that they had given me. I was more than willing to share my views, my lifestyle and the methods I used to stop cancer from swallowing up my positivity. It was a short but powerful story that I compiled.

A few days later, the RDH media team called to say that they wanted to enhance my success story and share it on the hospital website. This I was thrilled about as I wanted as many women as possible to be aware of cervical cancer.

The gentleman went on to ask whether he could share my photos and the information he had just gathered from me. He mentioned that other media sites would be able to view what he was going to write up and post, such as Twitter and Instagram. I replied, "The more who read my story, the better — that's the whole point!" I hung up the call and thought no more of it.

In the evening, I looked on Facebook out of curiosity to see how many followed the hospital page, and I was stunned to see the figure of 29k. It hit me there and then that a lot of people would engage with my views.

On 24th April my father-in-law sent me a link. I clicked on it — it was a live media article all about my journey! I was pleased, to say the least. It was funny. It felt humbling. The link was on Derbyshire Live News.

I went to my friend's house and drank tea all day outside; we were chin-wagging and catching up. I told her about the link, as I was so happy awareness was moving around the internet. She said that she would check it out and have a read. As I drove home, I did wonder if it might be in a newspaper, but returned home and forgot to nip to the shops to look at the news stand.

I walked into my house and Richard had tea under control (steak, chips and peas) so I asked him, "Could I pop out and see if my article is somewhere in a newspaper?" He replied, "Yes, no problem — you go."

I went to my local Ilkeston Tesco Extra and managed to pick up the very last newspaper, The Derbyshire Telegraph. I walked to the end of the display stand to see if I could find an article. I thought to myself, "I'm not buying this paper if I'm not in it!" I was expecting a small, pitiful article that was going to be difficult to find. There I stood and opened the paper. I almost fell over with shock! I'd only gone and made page 3! My story had been printed right at the front of the bloody paper and a full page spread to boot! It was madness. As I queued to pay for the newspaper, I felt like saying to the folk behind me in the queue, "Look at this! I'm in the paper! That's me!" I was beaming with pride. I drove home proud and thrilled. I was bursting to show Richard. Into my house I dashed and opened up the paper. "Look at that! I've made page 3!" I exclaimed, and chuckled.

On that very same day but before the newspaper shock, BBC East Midlands News had also called me on the way home from my friend's house. A gentleman had informed me that they wanted to come to my garden and do a TV interview! It really was a top day. It was a double whammy what happened to me that day. I just couldn't believe my luck!

The BBC gentleman who I'd had the phone call with had arranged with me that the camera crew would be coming on the Sunday of that very same week, along with a well-known reporter. I was over the moon. This news channel, I later discovered, gets over 200,000 viewers; I was dumbfounded at how many people would be watching my story and taking notice of the dangers of ladies missing their smear tests. It felt absolutely brilliant to be making such a difference to ladies' future health.

Oh my God, here it was. 25th April 2021. The day the BBC knocked on my front door! I was super excited, but I wasn't nervous. I had so much to say and share with the reporter. I was buzzing that my chance had arrived to spread the word of my journey far and wide. That cervical screening is there to save women's lives and that plenty of women put this screening on the back burner. I was also wanting to say on hundreds of thousands of people's teatime TV screens that "Men should be asking the beloved ladies in their lives, are you up to date with your cervical screening appointments?"

It was a sunny day, and the garden was immaculate. I had been out there busting a gut to make it look tip-top! Can you imagine, it's every gardener's dream to get their garden on TV. Again, another double whammy for me: to spread the word and to show off my beloved baby, my garden. I was flitting around with glee. All this on top of my story making the paper and having my health back.

I couldn't wait to get going with the interview. I had even made notes for the BBC presenter on my journey and some dates so that he would be well informed for the questions he was going to ask me. I was hot to trot, make-up on, nails painted, smartly dressed and sitting with bags of time to spare.

I had messaged Martina to tell her I was going to wear the blouse that was her favourite from a photo that I had sent her months before. She had remarked how nice the blouse was and how well I looked wearing it. So, when I chose my TV outfit, I knew exactly which hanger my right hand was going to pick: the one that had my friend's approval all over it — this was the least I could do for my dear, now very sick, suffering friend. I WhatsApped her a brief video saying tell me now if you don't want me to say hi to you on the BBC, but she wasn't getting back to me. I was hoping she was going to be alright with me mentioning her name on the news, as she hadn't confirmed this to me. In my mind I was thinking that she hadn't got long now until she moved into the end stages of her battle, and I wanted to mention her name on TV so desperately.

There I sat, spilling out my story, spilling out my heart, my mind overflowing with information. I covered the things I felt were important to share: to thank my family and friends, to strongly promote going for your smear check-ups, to say thank you to the Royal Derby Hospital, and to say hi to my friend Martina. All this on top of answering the questions that came thick and fast from the presenter.

This day was incredible. I thought that the film crew would be at my house for half an hour or so, but I had so much to say. The crew stayed for two hours gathering information. I told them that I had been looking after the birds on the village green, about the bird station that I'd focussed on through my journey, so they went on to film me putting some birdseed into the trays and compiled a great piece that was used for social media. It was clever how they used the information collected in the time frame.

The presenter asked me whether cancer had changed me and I replied, "No, not really", but looking back, it had. It had made me very humble and also a lot more focussed, but I didn't know it yet!

I gave Martina my humble friendly gesture — a very small, memorable, personal gift from this glowing opportunity that I was so lucky to have been given. I was delighted that she witnessed me acknowledging her as I waved and said "Hello Martina" on BBC TV. Thousands heard her beautiful name, and I am so pleased that this part of the interview was aired — it was really important to me. I shared with the reporter that very day of filming the TV piece on my lawn that I had found my golden angel, who was now losing her battle.

Martina messaged me before the teatime interview was aired, asking how I was feeling about being on TV. I replied, "I hope I don't come across as a right idiot in front of thousands of people watching the interview!" She laughed.

She said afterwards that I was so natural on TV and thanked me for saying hello to her. Had the boot been on the other foot, I would have loved her to say hi to me on TV. I would have viewed this as a great honour, and she did too — she loved it.

Dawn

I am writing this on the evening that the TV crew visited my house. It is 25th April 2021. My mam, Dawn, would be so proud of me — she would have loved seeing all these things unfold. She would have absolutely 100% supported me so much today, the day the TV people arrived at my door. I can just imagine that she would have been super thrilled to be the tea lady looking after the crew and seeing her daughter in all her glory, cancer-free, confidently pushing forwards with her plight to spread cervical cancer awareness. She would have most definitely been in my bedroom, looking out of my bedroom doors up into my garden and lapping up what was happening to me on the lawn. She would have been taking photos, I'm sure, marking how proud she felt of this moment.

What a fabulous supportive parent she was. Everything I have offered up as a mum to my own two children is all down to her mentoring. When I owned the little flower shop, I would leave a staff member in charge some days, and the freedom of mother and daughter shopping days would unfold. I am very much like my mam, wearing my heart on my sleeve and loving a good challenge.

My mam was very creative and could really turn water into

wine. When I was four, I can remember her coming home, through the kitchen door, full of smiles. She was on cloud nine as she had passed her driving test. I remember my dad burnt the tea that night just as she returned home.

Driving gave her freedom, and before long she started up her own little business. A party plan idea, where she would go to houses and sell ladies t-shirts and jumpers. She found her target market in the school playground and offered the willing mums commission on the sales made in people's living rooms on those nights. I can just about remember going with her a few times to do this.

This soon gave her enough money to buy more stock, and she purchased a white Sherpa van and started doing market stalls three times a week. This she loved. It was her empire and her pride; it gave her purpose and pocket money. My mam Dawn was so very dedicated, although her worst trait was not being good at getting up in the mornings, something that she has passed down to me unfortunately.

My mam ran this business from the age of me being 5 until I was 15, I would estimate, as she used to pick me up from secondary school in her van. By then, my dad had bought her a sunflower yellow Volkswagen van and my sister and I hated the colour. My mam wasn't impressed either as she loved her old Sherpa van so much. It was on its last legs by then though, so a change was the only option. Mam didn't have this van long — she soon had a different white van, this time a Transit.

Markets by then were booming; it was back in the day when all market squares were packed with stalls. Mam would have to queue up alongside other market traders to see if she would be allocated a stall, and if she arrived later than 8.30 a.m. then she ran the risk of not doing business that day. Her business was called "Dawn's Tops". It seems like yesterday that she would let me help her stamp the brown paper bags. It was a rubber stamp with an ink pad, and I felt so important doing this job when I was little. The stamped bag acted as a customer receipt as there was another stallholder on the market also selling the same stock, and this was Mam's genius way of proving whether a customer had bought the clothing from her stall. If people wanted a refund for a jumper that didn't fit and it was returned in the stamped bag, then this was Mam's sure way of knowing that it was definitely her stock.

She had a wooden box for a till that my grandad had made her, and she used to hide this under the row of jumpers nearest to where she stood and served. I loved to help her count the day's takings, especially at Christmas times. Our family living room carpet would be totally covered in bank notes. It was magical to witness as a child. It really put the buzz into Christmas back in the 1980s and early 1990s as I looked at the hundreds of pounds that my mam would pull out from every pocket and hiding place she had in her trousers and coat. Mam would then let me neaten up the huge pile of crumpled up notes and encourage me to count them — what a great maths teacher she was too!

My sister and I always had brilliant Christmas gifts due to my mam's hard work. My dad had a good job too. He worked at Linby colliery at the pit, fixing locomotion trains. This he did for about 15 years, and he absolutely adored it.

The markets Mam did offer me such fantastic memories. She

used to give me my weekly family allowance and I was able to walk around Mansfield and treat myself to whatever I spotted. She did this as a sweetener, as I had to go to work with her every Saturday as my dad was at work.

I loved helping her set up the stall. We would unload all her stock, then she'd leave me in charge whilst she went off to park her van a five-minute drive away. When she returned, I had started hanging jumpers the way that it was set out every week. Gosh, she was an amazing inspiration. What a start she gave me; what an insight she showed me into what it's like to be driven and work hard. She gave me a love of seeing lots of money, which pushed me forward to own my own business. She showed me such strong ropes.

I hated school and she used to threaten me that if I wasn't attending, then I'd have to go to market with her. This I loved — I got to bunk off school and be with my best friend and role model. She'd pay me too at the end of the day, so there was nothing to lose apart from my education, ha-ha!

As she was always running late, she would drive really fast to get to Mansfield and queue for her pitch. Her driving would sometimes scare me. I even remember being about the age of 8 and being poorly. She had to go to the market to earn money and I was ill, so I had to sleep under the wooden market boards. The cloth that covered the boards and all the jumpers above me, there I huddled up in this massive box with a water bottle, wishing I could be in bed at home recovering. My mam had no babysitters that lived close, you see, so her only option was to take me with her. The boxes that she used were grey and three foot square, making for a delightful cosy bed, the stall with stock all over it acting as a den.

When I was 15 the markets became less popular, and Mam knew she needed to source a new cash cow. This she had bubbling away under her hat; her new idea was building and growing. What came next was very successful for my mam and dad.

My mam and dad bought a static caravan at Weymouth when I was 11 years of age. We had arrived in our six-berth touring family caravan and ended the two-week holiday feeling so posh because my parents had purchased a large static caravan. It was very exciting at the age of 11. We had many happy family holidays at this huge campsite called "Littlesea". When I was 15, my mam gave up the markets. She and my dad had been buying more static vans over the space of four years, and by now the caravans were providing nicely. By the time I was 20 years of age my mam had turned a business of one static caravan holiday let into 11! These were fully booked every week because of Mam's brilliant advertising skills.

This was the era before the internet and social media. She had a real flair and it showed. She was very proud of the empire that she had built. My mam named her business "Milton Holiday Caravans". I can vividly see her now, picking up the landline phone and greeting every caller with this line. Weymouth was a four-hour journey from their hometown, and each weekend Mam and Dad would travel the four-hour trip to clean eleven vans. It was a hard task for them; often they did the trip in one day flat as every caravan was booked up and this meant that they had nowhere to stay.

My parents were both great role models to be around growing up. No wonder the streak of self-employment ran through me. The way Mam ran her business was a true inspiration. Having her as my role model made me excellent with money, and having good money sense is a game changer in life. As I type this story it makes me realise that the traits that drove my parents are also present in Richard and me. Because of this, our own children are also showing the same tenacity at such young ages. I am a true believer that what you see in your parents has such an impact on your own adult life. Dawn's — Mam's — tenacity most definitely runs through my DNA — cancer has proven this to me for sure.

My mam gave me massive strength and support when Trinity and Owen were little up until she passed away. I hope she had a word with God to save my life. I wish she would appear to me in some way or another; I most desperately miss her with all of my heart. The only good thing that would have come out of my treatment not working would have been the opportunity to see my beautiful angel — Mam — waiting for me in the bright white light as I slipped away from my family and this blessed world we have the opportunity to make memories in. I didn't want to leave this world, but the only consolation was seeing this stunning woman in heaven waiting there to welcome me warmly.

I am 45 but I still miss my mam. All daughters need a mum by their side — it's just a fact. I shall do everything I can, health and lifestyle-wise, to fight to give this gift to my daughter and son, although I think daughters need a mum much more than lads do — no offence, Owen!

I have driven to a place that is very special to me —

Whatstandwell, in Matlock. This is where my mam passed away in December 2003. Maybe this was the set path as her passing made me so strong and I had to be tough, and quick about it. Maybe the passing of my mam prepared me for the biggest fight — life — and gave me strength and true grit for my body and mind. If that was the plan, then it worked!

Behind me is the river. It sounds so gentle, so calming — a perfect place to round up my perfect day. My beast waits in the car park in the far distance. Another trip out in my car; it has been part of another crazy emotional experience. The TV people landing in my back garden, of all things! There it sits in the distance, watching over me as I write this chapter all about my beautiful dear Mam.

All I can hear is water slapping against the huge rocks at the river's edge. Gosh, it is so peaceful here. I am reflecting on how bloody lucky I am to be able to sit here and soak up this gorgeous April evening. It is now 7 p.m. and there's nobody about, nobody at all. Where I am sitting, the river rushes by and there is a small amount of traffic on the road that leads into Matlock. Only me, this bench and my pen moving forwards as I capture this extraordinary day in my diary. I can hear the birdsong, which is so delightful. It's as if they are singing me a "well done" chorus.

I am so happy with today's interview. It will go on TV in people's living rooms, and thousands of families will watch my shocking story. I hope my interview will appeal to all ages who watch the piece. I even hope that people see the piece at home at teatime and then go to work the next day and discuss it with work colleagues.

I just want to add as I finish this chapter, that if women choose to, they can take a friend when having a smear check-up. I was amazed to hear this, but thought it was a great idea if you are feeling anxious about going for a cervical screening check-up on your own.

On TV

Tuesday 27th April 2021 — this is the day that I had been told that my interview was being aired on BBC TV!

I had been told that there might be a small slot showing at breakfast time if there was no traffic news to report, a longer slot at lunchtime, and the main interview would be shown in the teatime bulletin.

I'd set my alarm for 5.30 a.m. In a very excited state, I jumped out of bed, keen to see the BBC East Midlands interview. I wondered which bits of material they had used from my garden interview. I had such a mixed bag of emotions regarding going on the television. Pride, fear, excitement and dread — in case I came across as a moron, ha-ha!

I had not seen any previews to watch beforehand; therefore, I, along with all the other viewers, would be watching the interview for the one and only time and I had mixed feelings about this. Once it was being aired, there was no going back. I was curious and nervous as you can imagine — had I done a good enough job of being interviewed by mainstream TV? Thousands of people were going to be tuning in to take note of my story. I wanted more than anything in this world for it to be powerful and informative, and hoped that the BBC would use all the material that was dear to my heart to spread awareness.

My husband also got up; now it was 6 a.m. The news came on, and we watched with bated breath. The news finished; I wasn't on it. My heart sank. Now I would have to wait until 1 p.m. "Bloody hell," I thought to myself. We laughed and I turned my bottom lip in disappointment.

I had planned to meet my friend Joanna for a walk at 10 a.m., so off I drove to meet her. On the walk, I was laughing with Joanna about how early I had got up to watch the TV interview that I was proud of. We both saw the humour in how tired I now was. "Never mind," I commented. "I haven't got long to wait until lunch time, when it will be airing." Joanna smiled; we were both excited about seeing me on the telly.

We had a stunning walk over fields and headed to a pretty little church in Brinsley where the blossom trees were in full bloom, full of candy pink petals — what a sight. Joanna took a lovely photo of me standing under these stunning-looking trees. I look back at that photo and it reminds me of how excited I was at what was to come in less than an hour's time.

Joanna and I headed back to the car park. We stood and nattered a little longer, then on parting ways, I said, "See ya soon." Then I said to her, "You literally will see me soon!" We laughed again and jumped in our cars to return home; it was nearing 12 noon by then. The 1 p.m. BBC news was not far away and I knew this meant my interview would definitely be airing. I was on cloud nine!

I went to meet Richard at work and then on the way back home, now 12.30 roughly, we stopped off at Tesco to buy a meal deal and some bags of sweets for our lunchtime viewing! Ha, I was so nervous but full to the brim with joy that cervical cancer information was going to get pushed into people's living rooms. That women were going to take note and hopefully men were going to listen too, and have an educated lesson with regard to women's health.

We finished our lunch and clock watched. I got so much more nervous as the hands on the clock edged towards 1 o'clock. We then got settled on our sofa with our sweets and held each other's hand. Richard and I didn't know what to expect but it felt special. What a one-off experience to be part of.

The kids were both at work at this point but would be home to watch the teatime piece, and I was looking forward to watching it as a family. What a great thing, I thought.

The BBC news started, and I began to smile. This is madness — I'm going to be on TV! I thought. I was giddy with nerves. This was my chance to spread cancer awareness, to get ladies to go for cervical check-ups, to gain five minutes of fame. It was all so bloody brilliant! I needed complete silence so that I could watch every detail of the interview.

The lady presenter stood at her table, on the screen of our home TV. I was on my sofa looking forwards at our television, my husband beside me. She all of a sudden looked down at her notes and said my name, Michelle Camm, and then my face appeared on a TV monitor next to the presenter! My husband started to snigger in disbelief. "Shush!" I bossily demanded.

I felt on top of the world. My favourite picture from my cancer journey, me with my big, beautiful bow on my head, was showing on my TV screen in my own living room! The very same photo that appears on the front of this book that you are holding. My television had me on it! What the hell, it was what fairy-tales are made of. We listened, then it ended. My husband said, "Well done, buddy," and he held my shoulder and gave me a kiss. The interview made my afternoon.

Some of my friends were able to tune in because they weren't at work due to Covid-19; some messaged me to say how great it was. We were all very excited for the teatime bulletin — it was going to be more in-depth, we'd been told.

It was so funny; within ten minutes of me being a TV star (ha-ha!) my husband had me scrabbling around in mud and dirt to fix our next-door neighbour's fence that had come out of alignment. I remarked to my husband, "I'm a celebrity; I shouldn't be doing this, you know!" We giggled. We were out there until nearly teatime doing this repair job. Onto the next TV appearance, I thought. It was such a brilliant day.

In we came from fixing the fence. We sat and had tea, now united as a family. Both of my children were now home. We all got comfy to watch my next interview. My kids were giggling as we waited as a family for the interview, for their mum to appear. As my face covered our home TV it was so funny. I glanced at my two children; they were smirking. I thought how wonderful it was that we were able to watch this, all four of us. They said, "Well done, Mum." They loved it. I was one proud mum.

I sat there in my chair in the evening when everybody had gone to bed. I was still buzzing from the day's TV viewing and the TV was on in the background. I was writing away in my diary about how fabulous the day had been. I was also waiting for Martina to get in touch as she slept a lot in the daytime and messaged me late evenings. All of a sudden, I heard my name. I looked up and spotted that I was on TV again for the 10.30 p.m. showing. I was thrilled. It had been a great day for awareness. Thank you so much to BBC East Midlands.

A Lioness Broke Free

Thursday 6th May. A few weeks ago, the hubby and I went to Matlock for a ride out on his motorbike. A great story now follows!

As you know by now, I love the pillion space on my husband's motorbike, but for the last nine months, Richard had kept saying, "You should get your own motorbike!" I would constantly reply, "No, I don't want a motorbike!"

Backtrack two weeks to the third week of April 2021, we were sitting at a set of traffic lights in Ripley and I started to look over Richard's shoulder — what was he doing with his hands? I wanted to know what his hands were controlling and why he was moving his feet.

This began to make me wonder, why was I taking an interest? Did I want to be in charge of riding a motorbike? Did I want to sit on my own bike rather than sitting behind at the back? The answer was a resounding big fat yes!

Over the next twenty minutes of the journey home, I took in what Richard was doing with the controls of his bike. When we got home, I asked him all about how a motorbike functions. He said, "Why are you asking? Are you thinking of having a go yourself?" I replied, "Yes!"

The next day I called a motorbike training school and asked for information. It seemed within my reach that I could possibly be a biker chick in charge of the power rather than sitting at the back enjoying it! This got my hopes up. The penny had dropped — I did want to have my own bike!

6th May is the day that I purchased my very own motorbike — whoo-hoo! "I can't chicken out now," I thought. I paid for the 125cc motorbike and Richard rode it home for me. Wow, my friends were amazed. Martina said, "It is so you." I sent her pictures of my latest crazy journey via WhatsApp.

It is 8 years old and gloss black; it's a neat-looking little bike. I can't believe when I stand back and look at it that it is all mine, and that I'm going to ride up and down on it. How bizarre, but thrilling. It has a few bits of chrome on it, and Richard and I have decided to put a better, sweeter-sounding exhaust on it to make it sound more beefy. I'm taking chances and living life!

I have called my little motorbike "Dawn". Dawn and I are going to have lots of fun and adventures together. I have named my 125cc motorbike after my mam.

A few days ticked by and Richard said, "Right, let's teach you how to ride your bike." I was pooing my pants. "What the hell, though," I thought, "If I can do cancer then I can surely do this!" We live on a private road, so I learnt in the village. Richard had me weaving in and out of cones, and I was a bit nervous at first that the neighbours were watching me from their windows. One male neighbour thought that it was my daughter learning to ride a motorbike and he was quite taken aback when Richard said, "It's Michelle!"

I was concentrating so much on not crashing into things that I had no time to think of onlookers checking out my riding style! Or lack of it! When I first got on the bike, my husband was telling me all sorts of things to remember. "Bloody hell," I thought, "What have I let myself in for?" "I'm never going to be able to ride this," my grey matter gibed at me. I travelled about a foot and my hubby grabbed me. He said, "You've got to lean — it's a bike, you know!" I laughed. He had given my chemo brain so many instructions that I'd forgotten to balance, and he had to push me upright as I was leaning into his body. It was very funny, but he didn't look amused. I was just gripping onto my handlebars for dear life and felt as though I had taken far too much on!

I soon got the hang of it, and was loving riding Dawn in the village. Richard would speak to neighbours that came out to watch my progress. Neighbours would ask, "How is she doing?" and Richard would reply, "She's picking it up really quickly." I could tell he was really proud of me, his surviving wife riding around on her very own motorbike of all things!

Even as I write this, it makes me laugh out loud because it's such a great achievement and such a great story to share. Weeks and weeks of practice went by and I was loving it; I wanted to do it most nights. The thrill was great, but my bike didn't feel a patch power-wise on Richard's beast, although I think the fact that Richard's bike is so powerful compared to my little 125 bike did me a huge favour. Because my bike felt less powerful, it seemed no big deal that I was riding a proper motorbike all by myself, because it felt such a safe bike, power-wise. Dream big, peeps — nothing is out of reach!

The day before I purchased my motorbike, I told Martina that I was having her name on my foot! Yes, I wanted a tattoo of her name on my skin forever. When I informed her of this idea, this was her reply: "Don't you dare, and I'm telling you that in my mum's voice as you walk out of the door!" She also messaged, "I'm going to kill you if you do that!" She then went on to write that she loved me, and thanked me for being a fantastic support. I was set on the tattoo idea — it was a tiny gesture compared to the enormity of the love I had for her.

There wasn't an hour that went by that I wouldn't think about how she was doing or feeling. I loved her to bits. She was the sister I had gained in a seven-month period. I wish that our paths had crossed at the very start of my journey. When we talked, she would tell me how much pain she was in, and I felt so helpless. I loved being her true friend. When I stayed up late at night and she messaged me whilst I was writing away, it would make my evening. I truly adored her.

I wanted to carry through what I had decided with regard to the tattoo, so I kept the appointment and didn't mention it again. It was going to be my first ever tattoo — I thought that much of our bond. 19th May arrived and I walked into the tattooists shop and experienced my first ever tattoo. The pain was very scratchy, exactly as you'd imagine, as if somebody has a pin between their fingers and is working away on the same area of skin to make a deep mark. I sucked it up. I wanted her name on me forever —

forever on my skin and forever in my heart. The tattoo only took ten minutes to create, and as I looked down as it was completed I had absolutely no regrets. The area where her name was on my foot was very bony, so I could really feel the artist's every needle scratch. I had the tattoo regardless of what Martina had texted to me. The nice weather arrived and there she was on my foot as I looked down every day. Whenever I wore my pretty sparkly flip-flops it made me smile, because there she was.

My sister is on my foot; she is with me everywhere I go. When I put my socks on, I see her. She is always there with me, in body and soul. When I have a shower, I love to see her name on my foot. She is that important to me.

A week on from Martina's tattoo, I was in the shop again at the desk waiting for another tattoo! This time it was one for my darling Richard. He had no clue that I was having this done. It was a surprise for him; I had kept it a secret all week. I value him so much and wanted to do something so very special for him — something so meaningful, to say thank you. The words that I chose for my second tattoo had so many twists of relevance to the year we'd experienced as a couple.

The placement of this tattoo is something I had longed for over many years — about six, I would say — but I was never brave enough to go through with it. It was a tattoo on my spine! Originally, I wanted some of my wedding song words down my back, but now I had another plan. More fitting words came to mind, words that ran extremely deep, words that were so precious to me, words that topped my wedding song words! Words that were appropriate for what we had been doing as a couple together, words that explained the gratitude I had for him and what he had made come true for me. Words that summed up the fun and bond we both felt on the motorbike.

I was dreading having it done. I had researched that a spine tattoo is very painful, but it wasn't as bad as what I expected. I laid down on the tattoo couch and took a deep breath. I was having these words down my back for my most cherished friend in the world. I'd listened to these words so many times in the shower and sung them out loud thinking of my rock, and how I did not want to be parted from him. This small collection of letters, bloody hell, they meant so much to me. I'd used these words to lift me high when I was at my lowest in the shower. This was my favourite line in my survival song.

I'd always sing this line and think of me and Richard. The line reminded me of zooming round on the bike. The words were so fitting to what we had been experiencing over the past nine months. The miles we'd ridden together, the nine months of speed we'd enjoyed, the nine months of happiness Richard had provided me with, filling my sorrowful cancer heart. Each ride out on the motorbike meant building memories, sharing togetherness, and was always about creating fun in case I got worse — in case cancer killed me. My heart raced with him; my heart raced with his heart as I held him tight on the motorbike. Every time my arms were around Richard, I felt immense love and contentment.

I booked this second tattoo appointment on the day of having Martina's tattoo, so this was the second tattoo in one week flat! My motto from there on in: do, don't say you'll do. The words down my back are from my shower song, the best friend when I was wet and lonely, the friend that saw me breaking down in the glass cubicle, the tiniest room that saw me crack in the evenings. The song that hid my cries from my family, the song that protected my family's feelings. The words I chose to have on my skin forever for my husband were as follows: "My heart races with you". So stupendously apt for my friend, my motorbike mate, my love who made my motorbike dream a reality.

My heart races with you — a collection of words that are so fitting for my Richard and a biker chick's back and for all the miles of fun we have gobbled up so far.

I came home. He was eating his lunch at the dining room table, and I said, "I've had something done for you this morning!" He looked at me in a dubious manner, and said, "Oh no, what have you done now?" He smirked and I smiled back. I couldn't wait to show him my gesture of love for him. I lifted up my top and turned around. He read it and was very taken aback. His response was humble; he said, "Oh wow, thank you mate," and went into an embarrassed silence. I then went on to say that I loved the words and loved him so much, and that the words were so fitting for our year. Saying this made my eyes well with tears.

Reach For Tissues

This chapter's heading says it all. This is a super sad story to read, so go and fetch yourself a handful of tissues for your face. I am taking a big sigh as I write this; this is not going to be easy for me to write, but Martina loved me reading these book chapters to her and she will be loving watching me working away on this story, making progress on this book that she so loved to engage in with a small G&T at night-time.

The chapters just before the previous one, she heard them all from my lips between March and April 2021, although they were all a lot shorter back then. I was really only writing brief stories; the depth of the stories is something I've had to change immensely on each chapter as I realised that there wasn't enough detail to compile a book. My Martina was a keen reader and she loved to physically hold a book; this she told me on quite a few occasions when she was ordering items from Amazon.

I had only met her husband once, and I did not know if he would get in touch with me with regard to her well-being. I had only met him briefly on their doorstep, about 40 minutes away from where my home is. This was when I helped her out by taking some supplements to her house. She was desperate to try different things to rid her of cancer. This was on 20th April 2021.

On this date the hospital had said that they were stopping her treatment as they could do nothing more for her. She was in bits, as anybody would be, and requested that I help her find a quick supply of natural supplements. She knew that I had taken many different natural supplements and here I stood, well and cancer-free! She was now up for hitting them hard due to chemo no longer being effective. She had nothing to lose by taking natural supplements.

I had tubs of spares on top of my dining room cupboard, so I drove them to her address without a second thought. I told her I was leaving my house straight away, but when I got to her house she hadn't even been discharged from the hospital, so I introduced myself to her husband as he answered their door. I WhatsApped Martina to tell her that I had handed the pills to her husband. She video messaged me back later that night. That's the first thing she did as she exited the hospital, she sent me a thank you video. What a bond we had. I still have her saying "Thank you so much, Michelle" to me on that very video on my phone. I don't watch it often but when I do, it is there to offer me a beautiful fix of our then bond.

Her very last WhatsApp message to me was on 14th May 2021. I did not know this would be the very last time my heart would be happy that a message had come through from her. I was delighted that she'd made contact. She messaged me, "I am so tired now." After her message came through, I sent her many loving messages, but my phone did not ping back. What was happening to my angel, my best friend, my sister of seven months? We shared a bond only someone who'd had the mirror diagnosis could understand.

I was low, I was quiet, I was worried. I could do nothing but wait for some news. I knew what terrible message was on the horizon and it was going to crush me! I washed pots at my sink, I did my gardening, I sat in my chair where I'd started my diary. I worried about her path ahead and I feared it so much for her. I was like the owner of a lost puppy, running frantically to try and rescue it. My friend was silent!

We spoke so many times through the day, you see, that her cold shoulder was hard to bear. It wasn't through a fall-out though; it came from cancer creeping round her body, day by day, taking more and more of her beautiful friendship, taking her beautiful soul.

No texts popped up at all after 14th May so I wrote her a letter and also put her husband's name — Jakub — on the envelope in case he didn't want to open her mail. I'm so glad I did that. I wrote to him, pleading for him to keep me up to speed with regard to Martina's downward spiral. This was the best thing I ever did. I was torn though as I looked at the stamped addressed envelope on my dining table. Should I go through with sending it? His wife was dying and I was thinking of our friendship — was I crossing a line? My mind torn, it was a no-win situation that I was faced with. My thoughts were, was I overstepping the mark by posting this letter or should I do nothing and maybe never hear when the end had been reached by my dear love? I did not want to be a pest at such a difficult time. The choice was torture! I decided to post the letter. Little did I know, but this would go on to help Martina, myself and her husband.

On 18th May, Jakub messaged me to say that I could go and visit my dear friend. I knew it was going to be tough to handle. I went to their home, where I held her frail hand. I stroked her head and told her how amazing she was, and that I loved her so, so much. I kissed her hand and looked down at her wedding ring. That's when it happened — she opened her eyes and smiled at me! Her beautiful smile meant my journey to her house had been blessed with gold dust — the biggest and most important thing to me was that my friend knew I was there for her at the very end of her battle. I didn't know if she knew it was me. She was so tired, you see; she kept drifting in and out of consciousness.

The next day, her husband texted me to say she was thrilled I had been. She'd been awake briefly, talking to him. She did know it was me. I was content with this news. I heard nothing from 19th May for several days, and it was heart-breaking. I was just waiting for the final message to say that was it; that my friend had taken flight from this world and was now a true angel.

This message came on 21st May. The most heart-breaking and toughest message that I dreaded and had been bracing myself for. She had gone.

It has taken me nine days to be able to bring myself to write this chapter. Tears are flowing as I write this story onto paper; I have even had to take a brief break and pull myself together. It is 12.10 in the morning; I have had to find the right time to write this down. Wow, I loved her unconditionally; her friendship was so pure. I feel her passing marks the end of my journey.

Martina was a fantastic mum. When she was first diagnosed, she was really scared but hopeful that treatment would work for her. One day she informed me that she had bought a chemistry set for her son. She was so excited about this, for them to be able to engage in it together, even though she felt quite poorly at this point. She made a very jovial remark down the phone that the pair of them may end up causing an explosion in their kitchen where they were planning to experiment. This was the crazy side of her — oh, how I miss that. Everything about her was total sparkle.

She was a shy, private soul but once she knew that I cared so much for her, the bubbly and confident side appeared in all its glory. It was the ultimate honour for her to drop her guard and be herself in my company.

Her birthday was 18th October 1978. Martina was only 43 when she left this world.

She loved fashion, and Amazon was her go-to place for her retail fix when she was too sick to venture out. She also couldn't resist the pleasures of the Boots make-up aisles! When she was well enough, she would often say that she was taking a little trip there to treat herself. Boots was only a five-minute car drive from where she lived in Derby. Her make-up was always so subtle and beautifully applied, and she always had such a natural looking glow.

As she began to experience really painful days, which was around early January 2021, she carried on being the same caring, inquisitive friend, asking how my days were unfolding. This she put into practice until the very last week of her life. She was heaven-sent, and heaven called.

What follows are some of the things that my dear and perfect friend said to me:

(On hearing about the motorbike jaunts Richard and I were experiencing) "You crazy bitch!" or "You stupid bitch!"

(When I sent her chapters of this book via WhatsApp microphone) "I haven't listened to them yet, Michelle. I'm waiting till tonight and listening to them with a little G&T."

(As I racked up the chapters) "I am super proud of you."

(The day before the TV crew came) "Plug the book, my darling."

(On my TV interview) "WOOOW, you were so natural."

(On my motorbike picture) "You must be happy as Larry."

(On me being in the newspaper) "I love how you are spreading your wings."

These words came from her heart. She was so supportive, even though she knew she was dying.

Her love and friendship were like a box of secret luxurious chocolates on top of the dresser; every contact I had with her was like a handmade, posh, indulgent chocolate. This I told her, about two weeks before she died. My box of chocolates now sits empty.

Martina, you made my cancer days so bright; so golden. Until we meet again, my love.

Suzuki SV 650

I t is Sunday 29th May and it's 5.30 p.m.

I've come up to my summerhouse at the top of my garden. This is a really nice girlie area where I can sit in peace and let my experiences flow. Many a Biro has ended its days in this area as I spill its contents onto my page to write this memoir. A really good and detailed story can take so many hours to get right; for it to be rich and filled with passion, or tears even. Then it will take you, the reader, maybe ten minutes to devour each chapter. It's a great piece of knowledge to share with you, I believe. This book may take you a week or two to enjoy, but it has taken six hard months from me and many hours at the computer making these stories into the very best ones possible. Every second though has been like going to counselling, and I have loved the process.

As I write these stories, I can look down my garden through these clean, sparkly windows and see all my companions that live in the soil. It's a tranquil spot to escape to. My well-trained butler has just brought me a cup of tea — he knows if I can't be found in the house, then I will be up here profusely sharing my day's reflections. My beautiful white doggy, my staffy of 13 years, has just sat beside me too. She has somehow managed to brush past one of the garden's flower beds, and stuck on her back is a minuscule sky-blue forget-me-not — how cute! She is blissfully unaware of how pretty she looks, decorated with this speck of mother nature. Her plump old figure makes me smile. She isn't fat, but she has slowed down so much now, her old legs limiting her exercise.

Last week on 19th May whilst I was having my foot tattooed, off Richard went to look at a newer motorbike. I wanted to go with him but my forever gesture to my friend was booked. Cancer has made us both realise that the bike has given us a hobby we so dearly crave. If the weather is fine, we are out!

Richard kept saying he would like a newer bike, so I was encouraging him to look at them online, and he was getting tempted. Many nights he was like a little boy in a toy shop checking out motorbikes. I lapped up his excitement.

When I came back from getting my foot tattoo, he informed me that he'd taken the plunge and treated himself. I was thrilled for him; I wanted a go on it, and sharpish! When is it coming? When is it coming? I thought. I was itching to meet our new ride!

"When are you getting it?" I asked. The day couldn't come soon enough. Richard told me how smooth it was; how it was faster. My bum couldn't wait to meet the pillion seat! We went to collect it; I followed him in my car. We pulled up in the front car park and I clapped eyes on it for the first ever time. It was stunning — it had sparkly cherry red paintwork and was only three years old. We went into the showroom and sorted out the balance and the paperwork for the new motorbike.

It was time to walk outside and start up the new bike. Richard climbed on it and started the engine. He shook the salesman's hand. Richard pulled away and I followed him in my sporty beast. He pulled out onto the main road, but I couldn't follow him as there wasn't a safe enough gap. I saw Richard drive away a few car lengths in front of me. As I sat there waiting for my opportunity to catch up with him, my mouth and heart said out loud, "Good for you, Richard, good for you!" It was a fabulous moment; I was so pleased for him. It had been a tough year, so what a well-deserved treat for all his huge efforts. Every inch of that bike he had earned for the strength and love he had shown me through my illness.

We are ten days into the ownership of the new motorbike. It's a delight; it's as smooth as silk as we fly along and get our boost of happiness. The exhaust is like listening to a song that makes your spine tingle — it offers different tones at low and high speeds, and I love to hear it rev under tunnels and at the traffic lights. This makes my heart spike like a needle on a lie detector.

Today we took a trip out to the dealership where Richard bought this bike from. We sat and had an ice cream and a cup of tea. The day was gorgeous, and we took our leather coats off. We sat there and looked at all the bikes pulling into the bike bays on the vast car park to do exactly the same thing as we were doing — to chill, and listen to and enjoy the beautiful roars of other rider's exhausts showing off. Such a simple thing to sit there and do. We both enjoy this hobby and this place. The wind was wafting through our t-shirt sleeves and there was a smell of fried onions in the breeze, coming from the burger wagon behind us. We finished our tea, zipped up our leather jackets and climbed onto our newly purchased beauty. Richard pressed the start button and gave the throttle a quick blip; oh my God, it sounded sweet, begging us to climb back on it for a fun-filled ride home. As we rode along the roads watching out for the yellow speed spoilers, the sun was blazing through our helmet visors. I watched birds flying overhead and I held on tight to my buddy. I spotted one of my best friends — the round white sign with the black stripe running through it. Yes, the national speed limit sign! A sight for sore eyes to any motorbike junkie!

Thank you, cancer, for giving us back our shared hobby. It had been buried for many years, and without you visiting my body, I'm not sure we would have had all these fun memories on a motorbike.

When we were about 20 minutes away from home, I thought of my dear Martina. Tears rolled down my face; I could not wipe them as I was holding onto Richard, and it was impossible to get my hand up into my helmet. I thought to myself, "I must live my best life for Martina too now. My fun is for me and her; I have to grab every bit of life with full force and make her proud of me." I pictured her calling me a crazy bitch, something you readers possibly think too. Ha-ha!

Bittersweet

We travelled on our motorbike again yesterday, 31st May 2021; it was a bank holiday Monday and the weather was divine. We were thirty minutes into our ride and again, as I had done so many times throughout the day, I began to think of Martina. Tears started to dampen my helmet padding; the tears were because of this very special ending.

As you all know by now, my darling has taken flight. I am coming to terms with the loss day by day. The days are incredibly hard without my soul sister. It cuts deeper than I could ever have imagined it would. I have had three months to accept that she was going to leave my side, but even this period has not helped soften the blow. We are now ten days in since her passing. Every quiet moment that I experience I just can't pull myself together.

I have been in contact with Martina's husband Jakub every day since her death to see how he is coping. I reflect on my emotions towards her loss, and it can be nothing compared to his loss. The sadness and the loneliness that she has left me with compels me to check in with her husband and see how he is coping. My empathy for him is endless. We have become close friends in a very short space of time. The 18th May was when our friendship started, in the kitchen of their family home. That day I stared at the cooker, the kitchen sink, the places where I imagined Martina being a mum and wife, standing in those very spots happy and healthy, with no clue of her destiny ahead. This was three days before she died. This was the date Jakub and I would talk via WhatsApp about how Martina was doing. By then, she was too ill to get in touch with me personally. I felt so sad that he was at home with her just waiting for the terrible day to arrive. Poor, poor man. Along came 21st May. Our hearts shattered into an infinite number of pieces.

My friend Traysi asked when the funeral would be. "I don't know," I replied, as Jakub hadn't spoken of it, and I didn't like to pry. I felt terrible asking, but, like with the letter that I sent to their house that I have previously mentioned, I had to yet again be brave as I wanted to find out when the funeral was taking place and pay my respects to my beautiful sister of seven months.

Her husband replied, "I want a private cremation with no attendees — just something very simple." This, I now know, is called an unattended funeral. Martina's husband and her little boy of 8 years wanted to return home as soon as possible. Their house and lives were now stripped of love, and they wanted to go back to the Czech Republic where their main family lived.

Within these ten days of Martina passing, I built up a special bond with her husband, checking in daily as to how he and his son were coping. Once Martina had passed over, her family were searching for clarity and closure. All of Martina's family are dotted all over Europe. Her brother lives in Iceland. She had one aunty called Agata who lives in Germany, one aunty called Emilia who lives in Holland, one aunty called Eva who lives in Canada and a fourth aunty called Maria who lives in Prague. None of these family members could make the huge journey over to England. Covid-19, along with Martina's husband wanting to quickly relocate for a fresh start, meant there was no link left in England (apart from the ashes that I had yet to collect). My heart ached for Martina's two wonderful males: their house was now filled with death and terrible memories alongside a cavernous void of love that Martina had once unconditionally provided. Jakub felt he had to leave England as quickly as possible for the sake of his and his son's emotional wellbeing.

Martina's husband asked me to bridge the gap. Could I console these five important blood relatives and connect with them through social media to ease the pain in some way? I was honoured to share with them the bond that Martina and I had created.

Because they learnt of our deep friendship it offered them some comfort, and I am so glad that I could help in this way. Two of the aunties, Agata and Emilia, quickly became very good friends of mine through Messenger and WhatsApp in the first few weeks, and we soothed each other's sadness with the memories we were all swapping. I learnt much more about my dear friend through these conversations on WhatsApp and Messenger. It was a real healing process.

I went to the funeral directors with Jakub as his English was limited, and he was now separated from Martina, who had spoken and understood English brilliantly. Her job had been as an interpreter within the social sector.

On the day that we visited the funeral home, Jakub had been

selling their belongings along with his vehicle so that he and his son could return home. I picked them both up in my car and drove them to the funeral directors to plan and discuss the cremation. Another massive day that my sporty beast offered up its services to support my heavy heart. This time, Martina's widower was in my front seat. The lady who worked there was so caring and sympathetic, delicately sorting out all the details of Martina's final closure from this world. The lady who sat asking all the relevant questions asked, "Was Martina wearing any jewellery?" I replied, "Yes, she had her wedding ring on her finger." Martina's husband was very upset at this point, so I stepped in and answered the jewellery question for him. I had spotted a wedding ring on Martina's hand that day when I sat so very close to her at the edge of her bed. I had kissed and stroked her hand when I was telling her over and over again how much I loved her and how proud of her I was. The day that offered me a final taste of her companionship. This was three days before she passed away. Now we were about seven days on from accepting she had left our sides.

The lady at the funeral home asked, "What would you like us to do with Martina's wedding ring?" Jakub turned his head and looked at me with tears in his eyes and said, "You have her wedding ring, Michelle; it is special to you." We were sitting on this small red sofa together at the time. His gesture filled my heart with happiness and also crushing sadness; it forced me to break down in tears. He moved closer to me, and we hugged each other. We were going through the same upsetting hell together. God, I'm so glad he was my friend through these very tough weeks, and I know that he felt the same. Martina would have loved it so much that we pulled together to help one another. I am crying as I type this. I couldn't believe I was going to be the keeper of such a precious item. I hoped it would fit my finger and I hoped with all my heart that Jakub wouldn't change his mind!

I wanted to see a memory of her every day on my hand and didn't just want her ring, with the important promise it represented, to be placed in darkness somewhere for safekeeping. Days later, I drove to Martina's house to collect the ring from her husband. This is when I hugged him one final time to say goodbye and gave Martina's son a hug too. They had booked plane tickets home and were leaving in three days' time. I got in my car and waved to them. Another special friendship had reached its end. It felt like I had known him months, not weeks; we had shared the very toughest journey.

I arrived home feeling very hollow but also desperate to look upon my dear friend's ring and hold the item — the band of gold that she had placed on her finger every day to represent her promise, love and devotion. I slowly and respectfully lifted the featherweight white gold ring from the tiny purple box that it had been placed in. I felt such love and devastation and then a wave of affection. I stood in my kitchen, adoring this piece of my precious friend. Just a small circle of metal changed my life forever that day. It now sits on my finger as I type this memoir that Martina so loved to listen to and so desperately wanted to be turned into a book for the people to read. The only bit of her I could now touch. I looked in amazement at the size of the ring and I was pretty confident that it was going to fit perfectly. It looked a similar size to those in my own ring tray. Filled with hope, I pushed it onto my right hand, the second finger in next to the pinkie.

Of course, it was a perfect fit! I stroked my new ring with the deepest affection. There it sat in all its glory; it didn't even move unless I spun it round. As I sit here, Martina is glistening away, holding my finger tightly.

When I collected Martina's wedding ring, I also asked for Turbo. Jakub kindly gave it to me. Both snails now sit in my garden together, and I see them every day when I open my bedroom curtains.

Martina had been the main driving force in moving her family to England for a better life for their young son. After the day of sorting out the funeral, Martina's husband had asked if I could be the keeper of her ashes so that he and his son could return home. Martina had wanted to stay in England. Her husband felt it was dishonourable to take her ashes back to a place that she disliked so much. I was honoured and tearful. My heart knew straight away that I would have to find a special place to rest her. I asked Jakub, "Where did she love? Where did she want to be scattered?" He replied, "The sea." That is where I must go then, I thought.

She had a favourite place in her heart. They'd arrived in England as a family and lived by the sea for three happy years. Leaving the Czech Republic behind, Martina had been thrilled to view the vast ocean every weekend when they took their little boy to play on the beach. She'd longed to go back and live at her paradise place; the place that had stolen her heart. This is where she'd dreamed of returning to, hoping to leave Derby and set up home once again with her two special boys to make her heart whole.

A four-hour pilgrimage lay before me, to a place I'd never experienced. Not confident at driving on strange roads, I dreaded the journey. She was worth every mile though. Me, my daughter and my loving beast carried my angel hundreds of miles. I placed her in the footwell of my car, behind my seat. Taking command of her very last journey was an emotional undertaking that is unexplainable. I never dreamt in a million years when I saw her in the chemo bay that day that our paths crossing would lead to such an honourable journey. Through the still night we all travelled to reach her paradise ending. Not a soul was on the roads. We arrived at her ocean of choice at one o'clock in the morning. We parked up and slept in my car until 5 a.m. came round. Every second of the journey was a true honour. If her wish had been granted to move back to this place, then where I scattered her is where all three of them would have visited every weekend for family fun. Her paradise spot, the paradise image in her mind, was a breath-taking stunning bay.

Sunrise unfolded and I walked upon her dream sand. I walked to the ocean and could only hear the waves breaking; this was the only sound. My daughter and I were the only living souls on the beach. I was now holding my beautiful sister's ashes in my bag. I walked forwards to the ocean and laid her carefully in the perfect shallow waves. It was 5.40 a.m. Lovingly, the rolling incoming tide kissed Martina's sadness and it so very peacefully took her from me. Letting go of her and saying goodbye was as gracious and as careful as handing over a new-born baby. I will not name this place; it will stay forever a sisters' secret, but I can say that it was one of the most beautiful places that I have ever seen. My pilgrimage was a privilege and is now complete.

Since Martina's passing, her husband and I have kept communications flowing. Jakub and his son have now settled, and the building of a house is well underway. His son has found a nice school that he likes attending and the grandparents are at hand to help out with childcare. Martina's husband walked straight into a construction job once they had landed in the Czech Republic. This had also been his trade in England. A very dedicated hardworking man he is; especially now, without Martina.

Emilia and I have become great friends, talking every few days about the book release. Agata and I are also really close. They are both still coming to terms with the passing of Martina and also the lengths I was prepared to go to to free Martina's soul.

The story gets even richer with regard to the friendship link between me and the four aunties. All of them were so immensely overwhelmed and grateful that I carried out the scattering of the ashes that each of them insisted on sending me an international bank transfer equating to £130! They requested that I put it towards something of meaning as a way of saying thanks from them all. I was totally touched by this.

I shared with them what I had decided to spend their generous donation on. I informed Agata and Emilia that I had bought a trilogy diamond ring for my daughter, as without her support I would have struggled to carry out such a pilgrimage. This is something that my daughter can look upon and know the meaning of her ring forever.

I have kept the other half of the transfer money separate; it sits just waiting. I plan to put it towards publishing this book. What a great series of events, and how touching and spiritual it is that the aunties' gesture sits within these pages.

Penny

This story is about a purchase, four months before I knew I had cancer. It had been my 44th birthday and I'd set my heart on a posh ladies push bike, the kind that I could just jump onto in my pretty skirt or dress and go for a lovely ride.

Penny, I call her. My bike is really feminine — it's gloss black and has huge wheels. At the front she boasts a dark brown square wicker basket for my shopping or any bits that I may need to take on the ride.

As I climb on her in my smart outfit, something like fitted skinny jeans, white pumps and a smart jacket, it offers me such a feelgood factor. I'm not so keen on the sporty look on a bike, you see; I just want to hop straight on in what I am already clothed in, and not have to get changed into sporty clothes. This is a right faff in my mind, and that is why I bought this style of bike. Penny really suits my wardrobe choice, and the bike is right up my street. Mary Poppins, almost.

I fetched the bike on a dark night in March. I saw it on a selling site and I loved it straight away; I wanted it to be mine. Off my husband and I went to have a good look at it. As you already know, he is well into bikes due to owning a BMX shop. He was going to know instantly whether it was a death trap or not!

We arrived at an address where Penny lived in the shed. She was like brand new. I loved her instantly; I could just imagine riding on this pretty bike to the shops. I handed over all of my birthday money — the whole £200 — and home we returned with Penny.

The next day I climbed on her and regretted every note I had parted with. The bike was huge and high, putting me in a sit up and beg position. Because the wheels were so big and skinny the front of the bike was very unsteady and was wobbling everywhere. I hated it! "Oh my God," I thought, "Richard is going to say I should have had a test ride on it before I parted with all my cash."

I stuck with it though, and soon I loved riding her. It was just so different, you see, to the previous bikes that I had ridden. The weeks flew by, and lockdown unfolded — everywhere was closed. There was nothing to do, and panic buying was happening at the shops daily. My older neighbours were scared to venture out for fear of the Covid-19 virus.

We have a good friend who has a fruit and veg stall, so he came to our village to sell his stock. The neighbours loved it. We all visited him to purchase perishables. We stepped up in turns, as social distancing was in place. Richard's mum and dad also wanted items from his stall. We would hand our friend quite a few shopping lists that stated who wanted goods and he would fulfil our requests.

When our friend packed away and drove off, we were left with quite a few orders that were for Richard's mum and dad and their neighbours who all lived on the same close. We would load up Penny and cycle the fruit and veg three miles down the road.

Sometimes we would cycle along the canal. March and April offered lovely spring mornings, and it was charming to do the bike ride. It felt so good to help out and deliver people's groceries to their doors and also to offer kindness, get exercise and suck up the lovely fresh air.

Penny was right loaded up some days, but I loved it. Some days her basket was overflowing, which meant we had to attach another basket to the back, above the rear wheel. She was a right work horse; what a star role Penny played in keeping everyone fed and healthy. I loved it too! Penny offered so much fun until chemotherapy started, but then I had no time to enjoy her as I was wrapped up in getting well again.

When my treatment stopped, twelve weeks had passed by. I wheeled Penny out of my porch and cycled half a mile down the lane. I was suffering and was in such a worn-out state; chemo and radio had floored my fitness and stamina. I was so sad about this. I returned home 20 minutes later after pushing my bike the pitiful distance home. I was most subdued and downhearted that night as I realised what the treatment had inflicted on my faithful fit body of 44 years. All these years I had respected my body and kept in great shape, and now cancer had come along and I couldn't even do a one-mile bike ride without climbing off and pushing it.

Dark nights and Christmas time arrived, and I didn't use Penny at all. The following March of 2021 was now upon us — this is when fabulous health came back!

Baby Chick To Biker Chick

As you have read, 6th May 2021 was the day I became a true rebel! My very own motorbike was parked outside.

I was excited, but it was a very huge leap of faith that I was taking. Would I be capable of learning to ride a motorbike safely? Could Richard teach this old dog new tricks in the village where he offered me hours and hours of lessons?

I bought the bike, so I would have no choice but to become a real biker chick. Not just play around at it half-heartedly and just be a pillion.

Would this mum of 45 years of age now be able to pick up the skills and like it enough to follow her dream? The village where I had many lessons was safe and almost traffic-free with no real dangers. Nothing like the open roads and busy town centres. The evenings when I rode Dawn up and down were fair weather and enjoyable. My rock, my teacher, stood watching me, offering me a safety net in case I went wrong.

I booked my CBT test, which is a training day you have to complete to be able to ride on the roads with L-plates on your motorbike. It was approaching at great speed. I was very nervous. Here it was, 18th June 2021 — a Friday. I opened my curtains and the sky was laughing at me — it was bloody pissing it down! Dark grey clouds and heavy rain were in for the duration of the day, the weatherman informed me. I had never used Dawn in the rain.

Today, CBT test day, marked a year and two days since the hospital had plucked a biopsy from my cervix. Wow, a lot had happened in this one year! Could I add another momentous event to my growing list?

I turned up at the test centre. The instructor was late; she was stressed. I thought, "Bloody hell, this is all I need!" I thought to myself, "This is going to be a terrible waste of my time and money!" She made me nervous.

I made some errors and she made me feel really apprehensive. I told her, "I was just so nervous," and she was less than impressed with my response. It was grim — my gloves, pants and feet were wet through before we had even made it onto the public main roads in the town centre. Now it was Friday afternoon, chucking it down and school run time on the roads. Cars were everywhere, drivers were impatient, and my heart was in my mouth. I was still at that point where nothing comes naturally, and your mind is thinking of everything you must do for the engine not to stall. It's just like when you learn to drive a car; nothing flows, does it? Your mind is constantly thinking of procedures to move through.

She pulled me up a few times and said, "Are you alright?" My 45 year old face was so scared (that bit is really making me laugh out loud as I check my typing). I replied, "Yes, I'm just trying to relax. I'll be alright soon!" She looked less than impressed with my answer and walked off. I began to relax, and my riding wasn't as bad now. All the time that I was riding on the roads, my visor was up as I was wearing glasses for my sight. The lenses were steaming up so badly. My face was wet through from the rain and spray entering the gap where my visor should have been, but I just had to push on — I wanted that bloody piece of paper that would allow me to take Dawn on the open road.

She made us do this terrible mini island that was backed up with traffic. I had been round it the previous day in my car and it's really near a school, which doesn't help the traffic flow. This particular area that she was telling us to head towards was filling me with dread! I thought, "The Gods are not in my favour today."

We headed down to this island that I dreaded, and she asked me lead the way. I was not at all confident doing this, but it worked to my advantage as I didn't have the two other blokes that were doing their CBT test in my way. I saw a gap in the flow of traffic appear and I took the chance. It was so perfectly timed for me, and I entered the island and made it round with no issues. Blimey, I was chuffed! I thought, "What luck I've just received!" I pulled up and waited where she had told us to ride to once we had exited the island of horror.

I thought, "Yes, I've done it, I've passed! Now I can head back to the test centre and get my most wanted piece of paper!" Oh no, she made us do the island again. I didn't think I was going to be that lucky a second time round, but I was! A gap appeared, just perfect for my little motorbike, and round the island I rode, leaving the island safely. My heart was bubbling with happiness.

I couldn't use Dawn on the test as she wasn't insured at the time. I could only insure Dawn once I had my CBT certificate number. I rode back to the test centre on this well loved borrowed motorbike. In my mind, I felt that I had done a sterling job of dealing with the stress of the day and the awful riding conditions. I was soaking wet and nervous. Had I done enough to impress this unpitying female instructor? She hadn't given anything away as to whether or not I had done well enough to gain my CBT certificate.

We arrived back at base and pulled up. The female instructor who had been observing us through the day began to put the hired motorbikes back into her vehicle. Another lad and I waited in the rain whilst she strapped the training motorbikes into her van. We stood there like right lemons as she hadn't given us any indication as to whether or not we had passed the course. Were we going to be given our certificates? It was one of those situations where I had to wait for the outcome. This lad and I looked at each whilst getting piss-wet through. I can find the humour in it now, but on that day, she made me and this lad feel very unsure whether we had passed the course. She made us sweat for our results, that was for sure! We felt that we daren't say out loud to her, "Have we passed or failed?" It was just better to be patient and hope for the best. Thank goodness, we both passed.

The instructor wrote out our pass certificates in her stationary vehicle. I had done it! The drive home only took about seven minutes, but every mile of my journey home was filled with pride and joy. I couldn't wait to burst into my house and share my brilliant achievement with Richard. Looking like a drowned rat, I walked in, and Richard was in stitches at how wet my hair was. I couldn't wait to strip off my soaked clothing and have a celebratory cuppa with him. After all, I had come this far because of his excellent riding wisdom and his weeks of dedication teaching me the important skills. My wish had come true! I now sat with my hands around my hot mug of tea — a true biker chick.

There I sat in my living room, sharing the whole day from start to finish, telling of how scary and dreadful the test day had been. Although now I could laugh about it, as I was holding the piece of paper that allowed me freedom on the open roads — the very piece of paper that allowed me and Dawn to fully enjoy each other. The old Michelle, before cancer, would not have had the guts to cope with such an intimidating experience, but the new Michelle did just fine. Dawn and I could say goodbye to limitations. How bloody brilliant! Everyone was so proud of me, including Martina, looking down through the dark rainy skies. I feel Martina sent me rain that day just to piddle her pants and lift her spirits at my expense! I can just visualise her now, calling me a "stupid bitch" as her ribs ached with laughter, looking down to see if I could conquer God's elements.

Gratitude

These next stories that I'm going to share with you really make me smile, as they show that cancer affects the way that other friends of mine now view their lives after witnessing my year. My dark journey has touched others; they have taken valuable lessons from my hell. I am over the moon that my family and friends have put lifestyle changes into practice because of my illness. Here are a few stories of where people have gained love from my darkness.

My friend Mandy, who I have written about previously, made a wonderful change. She and her husband Lee always wanted to be dog owners; they used to put this on the back burner though, saying that the time just wasn't right for them. Just after March of this year, 2021, Mandy and Lee bought a rescue dog and called him Benson. I asked Mandy when I saw her that day — the day of the newspaper article had been released — what had made them take the plunge. She replied, "You — your cancer!" She said that it had made her and Lee realise that there was never a right time, and you just don't know what's around the corner. So, there you go, they grew their family with another member — a dog. A rescue dog that needed love and a comfy home. Thank you, cancer, you made their little family unit a lot richer.

The next story is about my friend Alisha, who I have also mentioned already. We were on a walk together one sunny day and we sat down on this bench; a pretty peaceful canal was where we had decided to stop and sit. She informed me that she had started going to the gym and also cooking from scratch, two things she hadn't been keen on doing before she learnt of my cancer.

I asked her, "What's made you do these things, then?" She looked straight at me and replied, "Your cancer." I was overwhelmed and felt very humble at her response, as this meant that cancer had also changed her and her family's lifestyle for the better, which is totally amazing.

I saw her again about four weeks later on 29th May; at that point I was getting really good on my motorbike but I hadn't yet booked my CBT test. We sat on a bench in a beautiful place called Victoria Park in Ilkeston. Before we fetched a drink and a cake we had arranged to meet near the flower beds, which is where we were having this conversation. There we sat on the bench in front of these eye-catching floral displays. She enlightened me with this next really nice story.

I asked Alisha what she had been up to in the past few weeks; whether she had anything new to tell. She said she was looking for a new job and that her husband Dan was taking his CBT test the very next day! I asked her, "How has that come about then?" She said that Dan had always wanted to own a motorbike and she had always stopped him doing so because of the danger factor! Then she said to me, "But your cancer has made me realise I shouldn't be stopping him doing what he dreams of." She said that she and Dan would like a big powerful bike like ours in a few years' time and that they both loved the thought of riding out together like Richard and I had been doing through my cancer scare. I was so happy that my cancer could now allow Dan to follow his dream. How wonderful.

I was also thinking about people who raise money for cancer causes. They do this out of love — maybe they've lost someone to the disease, or maybe they just want to do something good. My thought process on this matter, though, is quite bonkers! Think of the charity runs, think of the cake bakes, think of the packing shopping that children do for cancer causes or the many other things people do to raise money for cancer. Think of how this offers friendship, a sense of purpose, a sense of group camaraderie, a sense of goodness. In this respect, cancer stirs emotion to bring good to the surface. It's not just the money that is being generated — cancer is uniting friends; cancer is creating memories. Cancer fundraising is a two-edged sword!

I have just asked my friend Emily how my cancer made her view life differently. She replied with a huge list: she is now going to live life to the full, to try new things, to put herself first more, to take risks and push herself! Wow, my illness has really opened up her eyes in so many ways. She has taken so much from my dark.

My husband Richard has treated himself too, realising that life can change in the flick of a switch.

Thank you, cancer, for all the things that follow; hand on heart, I can honestly say that you are the very wisest mentor that anyone could be stuck with.

Thank you for making my marriage even stronger than it was

before; I didn't think we could improve on it. Today I broke down in tears whilst riding along with my two special loves: Richard and his motorbike. I held onto Richard and was hit by a wave of happiness and emotion; Richard's heart and bike have pulled out all the stops for me.

Thank you, your visit has made our family stronger.

Thank you for giving me the time that I had with Martina and the quest I endured to lay her down.

Thank you for giving my kids a lesson in worth and strength.

Thank you for my now wonderful bond with my three friends in the village.

Thank you for letting me spread awareness of cervical cancer.

Thank you for getting me in the newspaper.

Thank you for the TV interview.

Thank you for making me follow my book-writing dream.

Thank you for showing me and Richard our amazing shared hobby — the motorbike.

Thank you for making me realise I wanted to ride and also own a motorbike, and for showing me that I could pass my CBT motorbike test.

Thank you for my two tattoos.

Thank you for my survival song that I will always cherish; it has such meaning.

Thank you for my sporty beast parked outside.

Thank you for changing me. I am no longer scared of anything. Now I have done cancer, there's not much left to scare me.

Thank you. I see my life through different eyes now, and you have calmed me down.

What a mentor you have been, the toughest teacher that the bravest person would fear.

Thank you for teaching lessons to people I know too. Some of them have made big changes.

Thank you, because now I have to and am going to live my best and most colourful life until the day that I can't.

Thank you, cancer, for showing me how I can cope with the worst possible news. I have embraced how strong I have become because of you; I appreciate how lucky I am to have experienced looking death in the face and overcome the journey.

Your visit has made me do inspirational things that are mine forever, and nobody can take them away from me.

If your purpose was to teach me, then you have succeeded above and beyond.

My Care, My Questions

I have decided to write about the hospital that cared for me. This chapter is to say thank you for everything that they have done for me. The care and service so far have been faultless. On every visit to the Royal Derby Hospital, I feel such love and admiration for this lifesaving building. It is an amazing part of my journey and without it I would not be here.

I know the hospital so well now — all its departments and friendly staff, its clean corridors and its welcoming atmosphere. The many nurses, radiographers and doctors that treated me were superb. When I think about the front appearance of this hospital, when I picture its glass doors that thousands of patients walk through every day, I imagine a huge pair of soft squidgy hands lovingly inviting me inside.

These hands sit above the main entrance doors, waiting to give me a massive welcome home cuddle. These invisible hands give endless love and are waiting to embrace me at any point. This is a make-believe thought and something so tiny and irrelevant, but I can't help but smile because this shows how strong my appreciation for this place is. I want to say that I am so grateful to all the staff for all their medical knowledge. Thank you one and all at RDH for all your years of training, hard work and dedication.

Thank you to my two oncologists and all the radiotherapy staff, and a very special thanks to the brachytherapy team — particularly the three wonderful female members of staff who stayed with me by my bedside whilst I was waiting to have my brachytherapy treatments. These ladies did all they could to get me through the pain of being on that bloody bed for 34 hours. You all showered me with your kindness, endless care and tenderness. You three angels were totally ace.

I think cancer has been the toughest test, losing Martina the second toughest, and being in bed for 34 hours solid without moving the third.

Thank you to all the nurses who played a part in my cancer journey too. The nurses who took bloods and administered chemotherapy were all so upbeat and kind.

Top marks, Royal Derby Hospital!

I'd like to add a request to this chapter. I am not sure where it belongs in my journey sharing, but I think it will sit here just fine.

When I was accepting the thought of having cervical cancer and telling close family and friends that I was receiving treatment, a few folk I had to tell were a little insensitive. Just a handful of these outrightly asked me where my cancer was or what cancer I had. This really frustrated me as I deemed this question personal and insensitive. If patients with cancer want you to know what sort of cancer they are dealing with, then they will add it to the conversation for your ears. If they withhold this information from the conversation, then they are telling you in no uncertain terms that it is private to them. Please take note of this, dear reader. Do not ask where if this information isn't offered. A cancer patient can find it very hard to open up, so please use your kid gloves.

When I was first getting used to the idea of cancer, I would hate the stigma that cervical cancer carries. I felt that it sounded so dirty. Saying the word "cervical" made me feel uncomfortable. I felt that people automatically assumed it was because I hadn't been for smear check-ups for years! This did not apply in my case. In the very early stages when people asked, "Where is your cancer?" and I had to reply, "It's cervical cancer," I'd stand in front of them with an impossible choice: to be incredibly rude and say "Mind your own business" or to give up information that I wasn't then comfortable with sharing. It's not like I could say, "I'm not telling you that!"

I feel as though the cancer that I had is one of judgement, but in the end, when I shouted about my cancer journey boldly and proudly, I didn't care what people thought. My only aim was to spread awareness, and I am very proud of myself for this.

How Did I Cope?

I dug for inner strength — we all have it. It's whether we choose to use it, that's what makes the difference. It's not a special power that only I hold within me. We are all capable of being strong-willed. For strength I was so grateful. I feel I first used this strength when my mam took her own life. I was only 26 when this happened. I had to cope without her by my side. Because she took this path, I didn't say goodbye and the shock was horrific; it hit me like a high-speed train. All of a sudden, I had lost my best female friend that had been my world for 26 years.

In the daytimes I was left standing with two small demanding children, Richard at work and the gaping hole of my mam not visiting me through the days to offer her love and support. It was difficult, dreadful, and as mammoth as cancer: a young toddler, a crying baby and having to accept Mam's suicide. Also piled on top of all this were the grief and the lonesomeness that her passing caused in my daily life. You would think that depression was imminent for me, but it wasn't. Trinity and Owen were my anchor through the days, and they needed me not to disintegrate.

I took the view that I would show my mam each and every day what a fabulous job she had done of raising me, her youngest daughter. This period of my life at the age of 26 revealed to me the amount of tenacity and courage that my mam had handed to me throughout my upbringing. When her suicide darkened my door, my daughter was two and my son a baby of six months.

My best friend of 26 years had vanished without warning. As my very young children grew up, our little unit of four — Richard, myself and our two tiny tots — became very tight-knit; we were forced to pull together and find strength as a family. It was a new chapter, and Richard had to demonstrate his wall of strength back then too.

A couple of years ticked by, with Richard acting as the main breadwinner whilst the kids grew into lovely youngsters. On Owen's third birthday I made him a treasure chest cake and the cake-making business took off. Often the kids would have to tag along to work with us when they were young, as my husband and I did coaching days with BMX bikes in the summer holidays. Trinity and Owen were 5½ and 4 years of age then. These were often challenging days, as girls would turn up to these fun days wearing flip flops and want to ride the obstacle course that Richard had set up! Out of all the footwear they could attend in, they'd choose flip flops, wanting to ride up ramps and moving see-saws. We knew it was going to end in disaster! Incapable young riders heading too slowly towards the fun obstacles laid out. I'm sure you can imagine how trying a day this was! A repeated queue of the same aged kids all making the same errors when it was their turn.

We carried out these days as a family unit, with Richard and I trying to involve Trinity and Owen through the day as much as possible, but it was tricky to please them and work at the same time. We muddled through this, but it was hard going. It was every day for six weeks solid. Sometimes it was very difficult to work all day and also keep the children entertained as they used to get bored, and rightfully so! On we soldiered though, as it was our living. Shortly after this, we opened the high street BMX shop and again we had a situation on our hands with regard to childcare. Most Saturdays for three years Richard's mum and dad would babysit them both; the shop was too long a day for Trin and Owen. We were and are very grateful for grandparent help. As the children grew a little older we involved them more in shop duties, which they loved — bless them both! Trin loved answering the phone and doing till work whilst Owen was a dab hand at building bikes and scooters. This era of owning a shop was brilliant to experience as a small family.

Anyway, sorry reader, I got nostalgic there! I had always been fit, not drunk much and wasn't greedy on the treats, but now cancer was here. My body was healthy — apart from the terrible disease, that is. I was determined to stay me; determined to stay Michelle.

My mindset through the days was "Don't worry about something that hasn't happened yet", although the nights were difficult. That's when my brain sometimes let me down, and that's when I visited my friend, the shower downstairs. There, me and my song and my tiny glass three-foot-square room would share the scary prospect that I might pass away.

I blocked out the thought of dying so well that some days I even forgot I had cancer! I put an immense amount of groundwork in to help my body survive. I did this by eating extremely well and stopping all things in my diet that I deemed unnecessary.

I pushed the cancer demon to the back of my mind in the daytimes as best as I could because it was not going to sit at the front! It belonged on the rotting veg pile, way down deep. I wasn't going to let it take my shine from me.

I did as much as I possibly could through each day. I stayed me, I stayed busy, I wallpapered, I did gardening, I went to work, I walked with my husband and friends, I fed the birds, I organised village gatherings, I drove my beast, and I sucked up the euphoria of flying around with Richard on our cheap 13-year-old motorbike. I wasn't letting cancer grind me down. As you have read, my days weren't slow; there was no time to ponder on the fear and black. My body was rewarding me because I was eating well and being a conscientious mother, providing it with every bit of goodness I possibly could so that my body had the very best chance.

I turned the black of cancer into gold. I loved hard and in bucket loads; I messaged my friends and met up with a neighbour every day to walk and talk and share my fears. I took love from whoever wanted to offer it to me. My family were an amazing support: Richard, Trin and Owen, my three humongous giants holding their batons with nails hammered into the end parts of their weapons for added injury. None of my family at home ever banished their coats of armour; their stance was as fierce as cancer's.

I had to be the normal me; I couldn't let my teenagers down. I wasn't going to let them witness their mum being a total mess. "This might be their lasting memory of me," I would think. I wanted to leave a legacy of a strong warrior mum and wife that was going down like a hero! If I was going down, if that was my path ahead, I would be the strongest ever me.

I was here to set an example: to be the bravest they'd ever witnessed me. I was the mum, wife, friend and neighbour that everyone was used to seeing — bubbly Michelle; busy Michelle. Just because cancer had chosen me, it wasn't going to change me. Of this I was determined.

Gosh, these chapters take so long. Such detail I have to add, but I have to spill my heart across this keyboard so that you can really know the real me! Don't forget, at the point when cancer was active and I was sucking up loads of poison and radiation, that within my pocket of treasures sat my three warriors at home under my roof. Then there was also Emma, Martina, Rachel, Emily, Joanna, Traysi, Jenny and all my many, many other dear friends that I told you about at the start of this book. Their messages and concern for me never stopped. I felt immense love and support. This was the key. Love is always the key, no matter what is unfolding; love will always help you through.

I was at the point in my life where I was content. I had been blessed so far with a loving husband of 20 years, two amazing respectful kids who have never caused us grief, and a job that I loved. When cancer arrived, my family and friends stepped aboard without a second thought into my huge dinghy and grabbed an oar, all of them angrily climbing in with one thought in mind: "Screw you, cancer — you're not having Michelle if we've got anything to do with it!"

I had arrived at the crossroads of life and I was smiling because I was satisfied and fulfilled, even though cancer was chasing me. I knew this was the time that I had to be strong and do all I could to destroy cancer's intention.

I heard a saying on TV and really took it to heart. I carried it with me each and every day. It was "Be your most colourful self" — and I know I was! How did I cope? I was myself and I was loved! I was not going to let cancer laugh in my face. Death comes to us all in some way or another, and I had no regrets about any of my life choices.

I take 13 health supplements a day — more than I ever did through cancer — and I believe these supplements help my body's immune system tremendously. I am also a firm believer in anti-oxidant foods. You could research anti-cancer foods to give your body the best chance. I still drink green tea to this day; I have been drinking it for 14 months now. Research does show that it's a great drink to consume. Your body is affected by everything that passes your lips — just remember this! Our bodies are machines; neglect the machine and at some point it could do the same to you! You are what you eat... and drink! Please love your machine. Isn't it worth having fabulous starting blocks in case you genuinely fall ill, as I did? Then at least your body has a fighting chance, and you can say that you have no regrets about abusing your body.

Once I knew how much trouble my body was in, I straight away took action and gave up as much sugar as I could and completely cut out alcohol. The only alcohol I consumed was over Christmas! I moved onto consuming anti-oxidant foods and being my body's mother whilst it was in the sickest period of its life. As a team, Richard and I have always cooked from scratch, and I think this played a massive part too!

I also want to mention the immune system. What an awesome thing we are blessed with! Reflect on what it does to your body when you are really ill, when people are in car crashes and when women give birth. It fights the trauma for you, and it heals you in such an incredible way. We should respect our bodies much more than we ever consider. Neglect the tool and it's worthless!

These thoughts often cross my mind as a survivor. Time waits for no man. Misery is our own doing. If you are not happy with something, then only you can change it. Boredom and regret are a terrible waste. Lose your inhibitions, because if you can do this, then anything is possible — anything at all! Like it states at the front of this book: only your grey matter is limiting you.

I made every possible effort that I could to fight cancer. The diet, the attitude, finding happiness in each day that went by, grabbing true and loyal love, finding releases for my sadness. These were things such as the motorbike, friendship, crying in my shower and asking my survival song to rescue my mood, my diary, and taking supplements to help my poor friend, my body. Every day I dressed as though Richard was taking me on a date. Yes, I wore my nicest clothes, full make-up, and one of my many patterned beloved bows on my head. All things beautiful made me feel stunning. Feel good and you are halfway there.

Of course, I didn't want to die, but I thought death was something that I could at least be in charge of if it came to that point — thank goodness it didn't. That I would get a chance to plan my wishes and also to say goodbye. Maybe the lack of control I had over my mam's death gave me the strength to view my own in some positive measure.

I love a good project, as I'm sure you are all aware by now, and I suppose I viewed cancer as the most challenging of all. The aim was to amaze all who watched me achieve the end result. I wanted to come out shouting "TA-DAH!"

Inspiration

What inspired me to write a book, I assume you'll be thinking? Many things — the first one being my crushed heart for Martina's path ahead, but then I realised it would also be my counselling to deal with the crazy ride of emotions. The euphoria of being cancer-free battling with the opposite emotion as I watched Martina deteriorate. I knew that she was terminally ill, but in March I had a snippet of hope, although I was really in denial. By late April I knew God was close for her, and the visits to my diary became far more frequent. The lines on the pages were like tissues for my sadness.

Coping with two vastly different scenes — loving life and dealing with her looming death — was the hardest pill to swallow. I found an old blank diary in a computer drawer at home and the book journey began. The stories were brief; not good enough or deep enough to compile a book. I had to rewrite most of the chapters at least three times to make them deep and captivating. This was an arduous task. But on I charged because I had promised Martina that I would publish a book. None of the stories sat in date order; the draft stories were just thoughts captured in a very untidy manner.

Then came the thought that, if I could sell this book, how could it not raise awareness of cervical cancer? Generating money for cancer causes from sales was my third focus. All of these causes really motivated me to push forwards. All my stories were handwritten, the folder huge — a mammoth task for anyone who would take on the typing role and turn my ink into something I could submit to a proofreader or editor.

My friend Jenny's teenage son typed some of this book. It took him weeks to type it as he was copying my notes — a hard and boring task. Thank you, Brock Warren. Brock then had to go back to London to carry on his education, so I got given back the folder of chapters that sat on my floor, part finished and a lot untyped. I dreaded the notion that I was going to have to finish the remainder of the book typing, as typing is something I am useless at. I had typed the first chapter of this book back in June 2021 and it took me four hours! As soon as I experienced the terrible pace at which my fingers moved along the keyboard, I threw in the towel and gave the job to Brock and paid him to start from the very beginning.

Now the folder was back in my possession, unfinished. "Bloody hell," I thought. Brock had got up to 26,000 words, around a third of this now finished manuscript. I was sure that typing was going to beat me! The date I got the folder back was 16th September 2021. This was a Thursday evening. The following Thursday evening I went to my trusty red lipstick and back to my red lipstick wardrobe door tally chart ways. The target was set; the lines now visible again but with a different target! I had 50 marks on my wardrobe door this time though, many more than my treatment chart, which had had 13 in total.

Each chapter I typed and finished meant that I could dash in and take glory in striking through a mark. Soon I was addicted to this. It really is a great idea that I have put into practice twice now. I started to proofread and paragraph Brock's work. It was seven in the evening when I started; I got stuck in, and the task was an all-nighter! I was sucking up the work until six in the morning. Now it was Friday and I felt like my eyelids were on the bloody floor, with my bed shouting me, "Get your bloody arse in here, you mentalist!"

Sunday evening approached and I was four chapters off completing all the typing! I just kept pushing on. My typing was electric by now, as you can imagine! I was on a roll, I needed to just smash it out of the park and finish! I thought to myself in a split second, "If I can do cancer, then I can do typing." My progress was impressive, I even admit it myself!

Anyway, from Martina, to spreading awareness of cervical cancer, to raising money, then came many other reasons to stick with writing this book. However, sometimes I doubted myself and wondered if people would want to hear about my journey. I also wondered whether my lack of writing experience would prevent the book from being a good enough read. I had thoughts of how Martina would be so proud of me, thoughts of thanking my family and friends, thoughts of helping and inspiring others, of maybe helping cancer victims view their path differently, and of sharing my experiences with other cancer survivors. As you can see, my reasons were plentiful. I wanted to offer love and a feelgood factor to all who read my memoir. To show that even with death snapping at my heels, anything is possible for anybody.

It has been so enjoyable for me; I love a great target. I want to show that even when your life is on the line, fun is possible, and you should make memories while you still can. I don't think it is a big deal that I have written a book, and I have thoroughly enjoyed the process. Apart from the part of having to type it up myself, ha-ha!

The words and chapters have flowed so easily because they are my truth. Like I said on the BBC news, I have had the richest but scariest year I have ever lived. I also said that getting the "all clear" news was better than getting married and having my children.

Richard, Trinity and Owen, I made this statement on hundreds of thousands of viewers' TVs and still stand by what I said, because without living I can't carry on loving and being with all three of you. Living was, and always will be, the highest goal of all, because without life there is no love, and without love we are nothing.

My daughter Trinity, my first born, is my pebble. Even though her birth certificate states that she is just 19 years of age, she is very wise. She is my shopping pal, and we have a very close mother–daughter bond. I am so proud of her — she is grounded, good with money and has a really caring nature; she is everything I could wish for in a daughter. I'm so glad that cancer is no more as this means that I can carry on supporting her when she needs a friend. Everything that she achieves is down to her true grit and dedication. I call her my pebble because of a Facebook post I wrote one day. This was exactly one week after receiving my wonderful news. I called her my pebble in the post because of her height and I also called her my rock in the same write-up because she was so strong in front of me through my illness. She's not very tall, but she's bloody awesome at football. On the pitch she is more of a boulder — firm, reliable and not to be messed with. Left- and right-footed on the pitch, she is every coach's dream player, and at home she is my dream daughter. She has such a kind soul, and all she has achieved at such a young age amazes me every day.

I can't really recall the emotions or how I phrased telling Trinity about my cancer diagnosis. My mind and heart have blocked out that horrific discussion. The body's coping mechanism is a powerful thing when tragedy strikes, and all I can tell you about how she has handled the massive scary news is that she has been incredibly strong — only on very few occasions did she seek out my shoulder with her tears. I know her bed and duvet were her crying cave; I can only try to envisage how many fearful episodes she must have experienced under this place. It pains me terribly to think of her lying there, terrified about my health, and it pains me endlessly to think of her young 19-year-old heart having to accept that her best, most loyal friend might leave her side. This is another reason why I had to dig my heels in deep and be so strong. We had many more shopping trips to still carry out, hey Trin?!

My son Owen is my sunshine. He is very hardworking, lives for fishing, and is a very loyal boyfriend to his girlfriend of three years. I have always nicknamed him "my sunshine", as he possesses a smile that would melt ice, just as the sunshine would. Thank you, Owen, for still cuddling me and showing me your love. I am so grateful that you have kept your word. You see, around the time when Owen was about ten years of age, we were having a beautiful cuddle and I said to him, "You will still come and cuddle me when you get older, won't you?" He replied, "Yes Mum, I promise." He has honoured those words to this very day and the hugs just keep on coming. Your sunshine oozes from your body, Owen, as you put your arms around me. Your loyalty regarding this eight-year promise fills me with gratitude. I will never take your cuddles for granted as I know it's not an easy task to keep a growing son so near. What a fine young man you have turned into. I love how you squeeze so many things into one day, working long hours then coming home. Back out you then go to fish, abusing the days through the week to the very maximum. You're only 18 years of age yet you have the right idea about the work and lifestyle balance.

I can recall one particular snippet of my journey when I had to speak to Owen. I was told of my diagnosis just a few days before he turned 17 and he had planned to go to London with his friend. I encouraged him to still go ahead with his birthday trip as at this point I had been told that I had an 80% survival rate. The day the Royal Derby Hospital informed me that my cancer was actually now stage 3C and aggressive, and that I had a 60% chance of survival, my son was in London fishing with a mate!

We returned home from hospital and broke the awful news to my daughter. It dawned on me that I couldn't possibly ask her to keep quiet about the bombshell I had just shared with her. My daughter and son are very close, you see, and I knew that Trinity would be speaking to Owen every day by message or text. It wasn't fair on her to keep my latest stage of cancer from her brother, who wasn't planning to return home for another three days yet.

I had to call Owen soon after I had spoken to Trinity. It was immensely difficult to break such news to Owen down the handset when he was so many miles away. It was agonising to tell him such crushing news then not be able to hold him close. The whole situation was so cruel on him, with our family support for Owen not physically possible. I pictured him sitting there waiting to catch fish, with hours upon hours to ponder and worry about the state of my health. I couldn't wait for him to arrive home; we all needed each other.

Trinity and Owen, please promise me that no matter what, you will never drift apart. That is why we planned you close together, so that the age gap of 16 months would create a tight bond. You'll never find a better friend than each other. Please grow, love and respect each other. This is all I ask.

In years to come, when you are both older, I hope that you read this page and still have your wonderful sibling relationship, because Dad and I are so proud of what you have shared up until now.

My journey has been TOTAL GOLD. I am leaving a legacy: this very book that my teenagers will inherit and be proud of. Cancer has given me the opportunity to become an author — to make history for the Camm family. My teenagers may become parents themselves and will be able to tell the story that "Nanna Camm wrote a book, you know!" How adorable; how can I not be grateful for my lesson?

Without cancer, this book wouldn't have existed.

Little Paradise

The little summerhouse that I have briefly mentioned is where I have sat and written some of the stories of this book. It has recently had a facelift. As I have said already, I love decorating, and we have some good friends nearby who always have a skip for their business placed on their land. It is always full to the brim of old wood, skirting boards and bits and bobs that are from flats and home clearances as they rent out and refurbish properties.

In this skip I love to rummage; it is the skip rat in me. I managed to make my pretty summerhouse so amazing out of this rubbish that nobody loves. I cladded the bottom areas of the walls, I added skirting boards so that my room is cosy and windproof, and I even managed to find a book of carpet samples that I have turned into a rug by binding all of the rectangles together.

I have painted the cladding a baby blue colour. All of this perfect little space has been created out of love and waste. Offcuts of my recently wallpapered kitchen feature wall now also have a presence in my paradise area. The paper reminds me of floral screen printed material; it even has little bugs on the flowers that sit within the wallpaper design. Such pretty paper; it has a white background with subtle images that look like they've been drawn in blue Biro, as if somebody has drawn nature's blooms onto a huge artist's pad.

This you will be shocked about, but in this little room I have a bath that my father-in-law gifted me. He asked, "Why do you want our old bath?" I replied, "It's to go in my garden." I have for the last three years had a bath outside on summer evenings on my yard — it's so delightful! I fill the bath with the hose pipe from the outside hot tap. Now the bath is in my summerhouse, and in the daytime it keeps a tiny secret and pretends to be a daybed! Nobody knows its night-time role — to offer me bubbles and total indulgence.

In the day I lie and read on my acrylic friend; sometimes I even nap without planning. At night-time it is my beautiful-smelling, inviting, hot trough of water with tea lights dotted all around it. Paradise by day and also by night. Even Tyla our doggy loves to sleep in the summerhouse on the rug that's made with love.

When my friends come round, I like to entertain in this space; this peaceful space is then my beloved tearoom. When it rains, it is the most magical spot in my garden. In this little room of glass with its plastic roof, my daughter and I like to sit and have a cuppa, play cards and even just chill and chat. At night-time it's an equal delight to reside in.

Night-time is when the fairy lights are plugged into the extension cable. It is our pamper spot up the garden and it is totally amazing! There we sit with the steam rising from the deep white bath, with fairy lights above us that give a soft golden glow. It's such a special place made from odds and sods.

Trinity and I have our speaker on low, playing songs like Mabel or Whitney Houston. It's our makeshift hot tub in a once-that-was greenhouse! This is my perfect haven, built a few years ago by my husband so that I could grow seedlings; now instead of seedlings it grows a mother–daughter bond. Here we sit, plunged into the beautiful-smelling bubbles, sharing our day's experiences and enjoying togetherness.

Totally Tremendous

History was made on 9th July 2021. The events of this date were weird; I could not have planned it better.

I opened my eyes to the July sun seeping through our silver satin curtains and reflected on the day and what it represented a year ago! Yes, it was a year to the day since I had been told that my life was in serious danger.

I went to work. I was really busy and soon forgot how symbolic the day was. We returned back home and had lunch in our sunny front porch. Six hours had passed since thinking about the immense year we had undertaken.

My husband suggested going out on the bikes.

I was now quite good on Dawn, and this was exciting. It was only the second ride out as a couple using both bikes, but I had been going out most evenings to build up my riding skills. There were beautiful sunset skies, and Dawn and I were exploring new places. It was incredible that I had got to this point where we could both use our bikes and follow each other. That makes me so happy typing this, as it's such a big achievement, especially given my journey and given my age — it's not really something a mum of two teenage children would usually decide to embark on, is it now?

I couldn't wait to ride out together — how brilliant! Man and wife, each on a bike! We got dressed into our leathers and got both bikes ready. Both bikes sat side by side. It was a dream come true as I sat on Dawn. My grin shone as my daughter took photos to show how far I had come. What a memory to look back on! The only thing I was and am unhappy with is that Dawn has to wear L-plates!

My husband asked, "Who is leading?" I replied, "I'll follow you." Off we rode, out of the village and towards Matlock in Derbyshire. God, it felt ace — my very own bike! By now I was confident at speed, and the flow of riding on the roads was coming quite easily to me. My muscle memory was improving, and I was well on my way to using the controls with little thought.

I was strutting my stuff on the highway and loving it. My aftermarket loud exhaust that Richard had fitted made my less-than-powerful bike sound like I belonged with the big boys who straddled their monster bikes. I was one happy biker chick, sat on her ride, wearing her slick red leathers with her exhaust popping loud.

Our destination was the motorbike shop where we had sat on a bench drinking tea the second time we had ridden out on the first motorbike, the MT-03. The very bike that Richard had bought three weeks after hearing of my cancer news. This place we were headed to was where Richard had said, "Get your own bike," and I had laughed in his face at the thought of it being an untouchable goal.

That day he had planted a tiny seed, a seed that didn't appeal to me at the time or even over the nine months of riding behind him with cancer. I was Richard's cancer koala on his back.

That day he had said, "Wouldn't it be great, buddy, if you got your own bike and we could come here together on a ride?" and I had dismissed him in an instant because I loved the back pillion seat so much that I had no desire to ride myself, or so I thought.

Four major events had happened since me brushing off that comment. These were as follows: I had changed my mind, I had found a pair of biker chick balls, I had bought Dawn, and I had bloody gone and passed my CBT test so I could ride Dawn on any road anywhere. How flipping mind-blowing!

So, we were on our way to the motorbike shop where the seed had been placed in my palm when drinking tea from polystyrene cups that sunny day. Now we were going to be sitting there admiring two bikes, not just Richard's. On arrival, Richard would be parking his bike up and I would be doing the same — I couldn't wait! The idea of parking side by side was filling my mind with confetti. This was the ultimate goal, the ultimate dream that I'd done all this hard work for.

Dawn had seen it all: me fluffing gears, me riding her into some bushes in the village when I tried to turn her round, me knocking over yellow plastic cones with her front tyre when I was practising manoeuvring skills, and me leaning into Richard on my first ever go! My little Dawn must have thought, "God, I've got a right idiot here!"

Two months it had taken me, to buy a bike, learn on it, and pass my test — not bad going, I thought, as it had taken three weeks just to wait for a test slot. I had picked up riding pretty swiftly, and

Richard was really proud of me. I don't think he could have ever in his wildest dreams imagined he would see his wife of 21 years on a bike, but here I was — I had done it!

Ten minutes into our ride we encountered some red traffic lights, so we stopped. Richard was in front of me. In my mirrors I saw this massive Transit police van pull up behind me. Bloody hell, I couldn't believe it! The lights changed to green, and it followed me. It was worse than test day, my every riding move and speed being judged. I was sweating. What terrible luck on this awesome ride out we had planned.

It followed me for 30 minutes and within this time frame the thought entered my brain of the news I'd received exactly one year ago to the day. Yes, the cancer news. This time last year my oncologist had told me I had a 60% chance of survival! I had been so wrapped up in what the ride signified that I had forgotten what a symbolic day it was too!

The police van followed me all the way to the destination we were headed to. I didn't give a monkeys, as the sun was out and I felt the business on Dawn — no police van was going to spoil my glory. There I was round swooping bends, beautiful hillsides next to me, the open road was mine to fly along. I sped along the smooth tarmac roads in my sexy red leathers.

I thought, if this police van pulls me up I'm going to tell them that this time last year on this day I was receiving late-stage cancer news, and you're spoiling my ride! And hopefully, if this did unfold, they would take pity on me and laugh at my bold comment.

The police van didn't pull me over, but it followed me the whole way to our destination. We signalled right and turned into the forecourt of the motorbike shop. Many men were sitting drinking tea and glaring at the bikes pulling in. To be fair, that's the reason we go there too, to enjoy a cuppa and soak up the sights and sounds of the beautiful man-made machines. Exhausts saying, "Look at me!" So much beauty coming and going from one place, it's a real treat for the heart and mind. Richard chose his parking bay and I rode into mine — oh, it was so sweet; there are no words to describe the way that made me feel.

I climbed off and removed my helmet. As I revealed I was a wife on a 125cc Yamaha, that was one of the proudest moments of my biking trips to date. It felt MINT!

What an afternoon it was to sit there drinking tea, looking at our two bikes side by side. Dawn and I had made it. We had really arrived!

I am the reason I can rev my throttle hard; there it is, as I flick my right hand backwards, the power and speed, the thrill of a motorbike, and it's all mine to apply on the roads. Dawn is only a 125cc engine but she's fast enough for a middle-aged cancer survivor and that's good enough for me.

As I fly along at 60 mph I certainly have no regrets.

The Last for Now — Who Knows What Will Follow?

S o, this was my incredible journey with unconditional love by my side. A loved one can be your family, your friend, your neighbour, or anybody you bring sunshine to. You can be loved by many if you are genuine.

This book was born on 16th March 2021 from an innocent A5 diary. All the tears from that day forward were because I was losing my soul sister. It was the incredible day of receiving my "all clear from cancer" news, yet I was devastated because I knew it was the total opposite for Martina. My £1 diary would mop up the next disastrous journey cancer had planned. I held my one-way ticket and got comfy beside Martina as we waited for our train to derail.

The diary was my counsel, my dummy and the one entity to confide in when I was broken and at rock-bottom. I always reached for my hardback friend when I was overwhelmed with joy or petrified for my golden angel. These two emotions constantly battled each other, confusing my heart every day. The reason for this was cancer.

My darling Martina, the voice recordings you loved so much

whilst sipping your G&T on your chair or in the bath are now in print forever, for many to devour and reflect upon. I will not be sad because that is a waste of you flying.

What a symbolic day it will be to touch the final product, this book. A journey of many months, seven of which Martina blessed me with her presence. Cancer, you have been my cruellest but wisest mentor; you have moulded me into a student willing to teach.

The pillion seat is an extraordinary thing. Leather and sponge, that's all it is. What it offers my heart and soul though cannot be replicated in anything else I achieve. If I'm on that seat, then I'm on top of the world. When speed and thrills are looming, then so is my euphoria.

Finally, and it has to be finally, because you are the most wonderful part of all: my Richard, you are an exemplary companion and husband, and I'm so proud to call you mine. I will never tire of being your sidekick.

Your heart, your love,
has saved my life.

xxx

The End

Epilogue

It is now 18 months since the cancer diagnosis came to light and almost 10 months since I started to write about my frightening journey. I thought a present-day conclusion would be enlightening for you, the reader. It is now mid-January 2022.

This is how I am now coping with the aftermath of cancer, how I'm manoeuvring the path ahead and how I'm accepting the new me with compromised health. The worry has faded, but this is something that I live with daily. I can't change my past health and I can't influence my future health. The best that I can do is carry on having a fabulous diet and nurturing my mental well-being. I try my best not to worry about a reoccurrence of the disease happening. Worrying about something that may not happen could have a huge negative impact.

Existing as a cancer survivor is like having a visible scar, now healed but a permanent reminder of what once was. The busier the days are though, the less I reflect on what could be unfolding inside my body. When I lay my head on the pillow in the evenings and kiss Richard's lips and tell him I love him, the pitch black still of night appears and this is when the challenging demons have their window of opportunity to overwhelm my grey matter. My taunted mind unsettles my tired body. This is when I'm at my most vulnerable, and sometimes these fears and niggles force me to climb out of bed and return to the silent living room.

I sit in my chair and let loose my anxieties and heartfelt feelings onto the lined pages of my new diary, my faithful blank listener. This second diary does not know how far the first diary has brought me; neither does it know that the first diary turned me into an author. It waits on the floor at the side of my chair, always on standby in case I can't sleep. It is my first port of call when my mind is in a bothered mood. My love for compiling my apprehension and unease is a habit that I cannot kick. It's such a vital need that I am driven to act upon — it helps me mentally and spiritually. I hope that one day, my daughter Trinity in particular will really appreciate me cataloguing this difficult period in my life. When I am no longer on this earth, she will be able to learn about and love the deeper Michelle, who is not just a mum but a woman willing to open up and share her truth and wisdom. I hope that she can draw from my strength and the path that I have had to walk. I hope my story will be a deep and meaningful read for her one day when she is older. I feel that so much can be gained from honesty, and this is one of the reasons why I wrote this book.

I am certain that I have now reached the point in my journey where these anxieties I have with regard to the return of cancer will not dissipate one jot further. My mind and soul are fully at ease with my new existence — I am a positive cancer survivor. I have come to terms with the prospect that cancer may well darken my door again, but I have no room for complacency, only gratitude. I am still breathing and here to love everything and everyone in my life wholeheartedly.

I don't hate cancer. I have chosen to move forward and appreciate each day. I am very fortunate to be here, and I must make every day count. When I can't sleep at night, it's because I'm reflecting on my brush with death and how much cancer has changed my viewpoint. Also, I lie there and think of how cancer may be growing inside my body again. This plays on my mind — this particular worry is my monster in the closet at bedtime.

When restlessness unfolds, my diary is there to confide in. The solitude of the very quiet early hours is something that I have very much learnt to enjoy and embrace. I love the peacefulness of the atmosphere, just sitting and pondering, soaking up how lucky I am that I am still here and able to be part of family life. When I'm kept awake at night it's a mixture of emotion, contemplation, indebtedness, and the struggle to sleep when "what ifs" play over in my mind, but at least I'm alive and awake to surrender to the taunt! A strange surreal summary, you may think, but it's a true evaluation of my thought process.

I find that once I have visited my diary my soul has a sense of harmony, and I am then ready to settle back to bed. Ready to close my eyes and reset my body to witness another spectacular day in this big wide world.

Riding my motorbike Dawn, enjoying my family, and following my book-writing dream have been what I have spent the majority of my time on since being in remission. One more secret to mention is that as soon as "A Lioness" was submitted to my proofreader I couldn't help but re-visit the keyboard — this time digging deep to write a book all about my beautiful mam. She is gone but not forgotten, and I would love to share her lifetime achievements with you.

So, there you go. I have used my year extremely wisely, and maybe another book is on the horizon, a book in honour of the inspirational lady who brought an author into this world: my mam, Dawn.

If you would like to follow me, please refer to the copyright page at the front of this book, where my Instagram and website details can be found. Here you will find pictures and information about my dreams for the future.